AZ WALES
Atlas Ffyrdd 'u

CONTENTS cynnwys

Key to Map Pages..................2-3
allwedd i dudalennau'r map

Road Maps............................4-67
mapiau ffyrdd

Index to Towns and Villages.......................68-81
mynegai i drefi a phentrefi

Town Plans, Airport & Port Plans...............82-88
cynlluniau threfi, cynlluniau meysydd awyr a porthladdoedd

REFERENCE *cyfeirnod*

MOTORWAY	**M4**
Under Construction	
Proposed	
MOTORWAY JUNCTIONS WITH NUMBERS	
Unlimited interchange **4** Limited interchange **5**	
MOTORWAY SERVICE AREA	**MAGOR**
with access from one carriageway only	(S)
MAJOR ROAD SERVICE AREAS	**ROSS SPUR**
with 24 hour Facilities	(S)
PRIMARY ROUTE _ (with junction number)	**A55** 15
PRIMARY ROUTE DESTINATION	**NEATH**
DUAL CARRIAGEWAYS (A & B Roads)	
CLASS A ROAD	**A48**
CLASS B ROAD	**B4246**
MAJOR ROADS UNDER CONSTRUCTION	
MAJOR ROADS PROPOSED	
GRADIENT 1:5(20%) & STEEPER (Ascent in direction of arrow)	«
TOLL	TOLL
MILEAGE BETWEEN MARKERS	8
RAILWAY AND STATION	
LEVEL CROSSING AND TUNNEL	
RIVER OR CANAL	
COUNTY OR UNITARY AUTHORITY BOUNDARY	
NATIONAL BOUNDARY	+
BUILT-UP AREA	
VILLAGE OR HAMLET	o
WOODED AREA	
SPOT HEIGHT IN FEET	• 813
HEIGHT ABOVE SEA LEVEL 400' - 1,000' 122m - 305m	
1,000' - 1,400' 305m - 427m	
1,400' - 2,000' 427m - 610m	
2,000'+ 610m +	
NATIONAL GRID REFERENCE (Kilometres)	100
AREA COVERED BY TOWN PLAN	SEE PAGE 84

TOURIST INFORMATION *gwybodaeth i dwristiaid*

AIRPORT	
AIRFIELD	
HELIPORT	
BATTLE SITE AND DATE	✕ 1066
CASTLE (Open to Public)	
CASTLE WITH GARDEN (Open to Public)	
CATHEDRAL, ABBEY, CHURCH, FRIARY, PRIORY	
COUNTRY PARK	
FERRY (Vehicular)	
(Foot only)	
GARDEN (Open to Public)	
GOLF COURSE 9 HOLE 18 HOLE	
HISTORIC BUILDING (Open to Public)	
HISTORIC BUILDING WITH GARDEN (Open to Public)	
HORSE RACECOURSE	
INFORMATION CENTRE	ℹ
LIGHTHOUSE	
MOTOR RACING CIRCUIT	
MUSEUM, ART GALLERY	
NATIONAL PARK OR FOREST PARK	
NATIONAL TRUST PROPERTY (Open)	NT
(Restricted Opening)	NT
NATURE RESERVE OR BIRD SANCTUARY	
NATURE TRAIL OR FOREST WALK	
PLACE OF INTEREST Monument	•
PICNIC SITE	
RAILWAY, STEAM OR NARROW GAUGE	
THEME PARK	
VIEWPOINT 360 degrees	
180 degrees	
WILDLIFE PARK	
WINDMILL	
ZOO OR SAFARI PARK	

SCALE *graddfa*

```
0        1        2        3        4        5        6 Miles
0   1   2   3   4   5   6   7   8   9   10 Kilometres
```

1:158,400
2.5 Miles to 1 Inch
2.5 milltir i l fodfedd

Geographers' A-Z Map Company Ltd

Head Office *(prif swyddfa)*: Fairfield Road,
Borough Green, Sevenoaks, Kent TN15 8PP
Telephone *(ffon)*: 01732 781000
Showrooms *(ystafelloedd arddangos)*:
44 Gray's Inn Road, London, WC1X 8HX
Telephone *(ffon)*: 020 7440 9500

Edition *(rhifyn)* 5 2004
Copyright *(hawlfraint)* © Geographers' A-Z Map Company Ltd. 2004

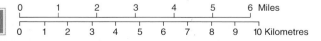

KEY TO MAP PAGES
allwedd i dudalennau'r map

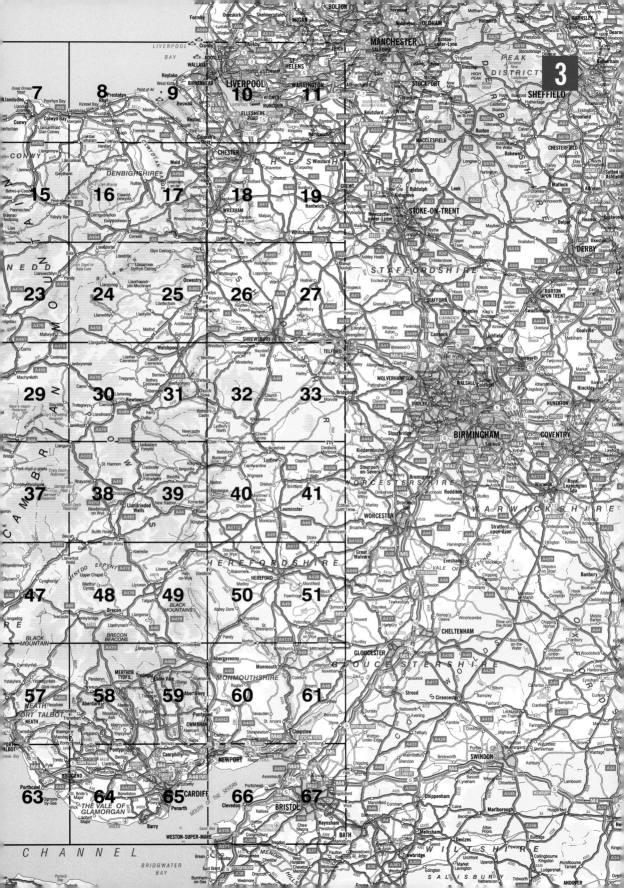

A   B

1

I R I S H

The Skerries
(Ynysoedd y Moelrhoniaid)

Carmel Head
(Trwyn y Gader)

S E A

Church Bay
(Porth Swtan)

Holyhead to:
Dublin 3hrs.
Dublin 1hr. 50mins.
 (Fast Ferry)
Dun Laoghaire 1hr. 40mins.
 (Fast Ferry)

HOLYHEAD   BAY
(BAE CAERGYBI) **Llanf**

2

Breakwater
Porth-y-felin
Caer y Twr
Hill Fort
Salt Island
South Stack
Cliffs
Gogarth
Bay
HOLYHEAD
(Caergybi)
Mountain
Llaingoch
Hut
Group
Stryd
Penrhos
Penrhos
Ellin's Tower
Penrhos Feilw
Kingsland
Standing
Stones
Hut
Circles
Burial
Chamber
Ty-Mawr
Standing
Stone
Trearddur
(YNYS
Four Mile
Bridge
Llyn Dinam
B4545

3
GYBI)
Rhoscolyn
St. Gwenfaen's
Well
Cymyra

Bay

A   **12**   B

10   20

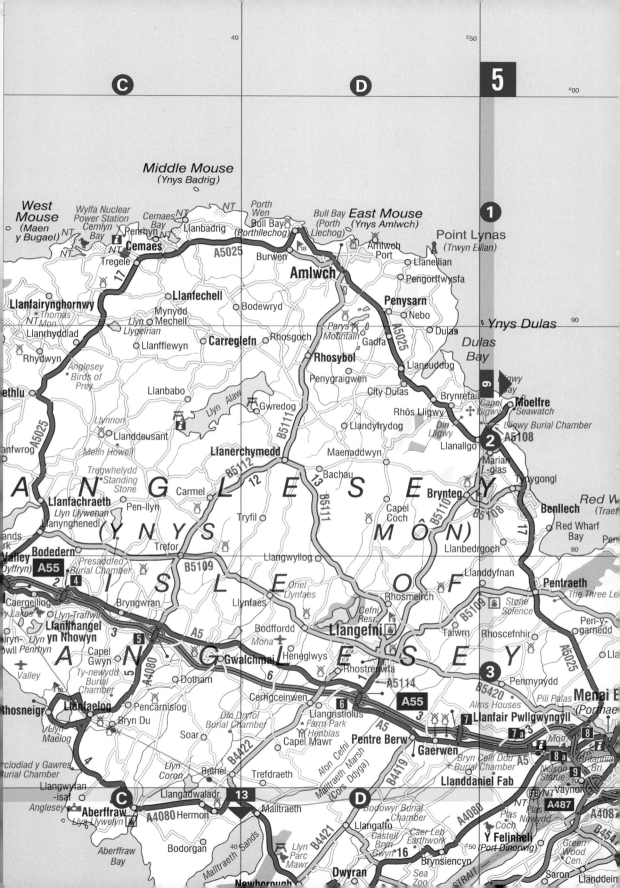

250   60   70

400

A   **B**

1

East Mouse
(Ynys Amlwch)

Point Lynas
(Trwyn Eilian)

Amlwch
Port

Llanellian

Pengorffwysfa

Penysarn

Nebo

Gadfa

Dulas

Ynys Dulas

A5025

City Dulas

Llaneuddog

Dulas
Bay

bol

aigwen

Rhôs Lligwy

Bryn...

5

Lligwy
Bay

Capel
Lligwy

Moelfre
Seawatch

Llandyfrydog

Din
Lligwy

Lligwy Burial Chamber

enaddwyn

Marian-glas

Llanallgo

A5108

2

**ANGLESEY
(YNYS MÔN)**

hau

Brynteg

Tynygongl

Capel
Coch

B5110

B5108

17

Benllech

Red Wharf Bay
(Traeth-coch)

NT

Puffin Island
(Ynys Seiriol)

Penmon
Dovecot

Llanbedrgoch

Red Wharf
Bay

Pentrellwyn

NT

Glan-yr-
afon

Well

Caim

Priory
Penmon

Cross

Llanddyfnan

Llanddona

Mariandyrys

Llangoed

B5109

Castell
Aberlleiniog

Penmaen
Swatch

Rhosmeirch

Pentraeth

The Three Leaps

Stone
Science

B5109

Pen-y-
garnedd

Llyn
Bodgylched

Bulkeley
Mill

Llanfaes

Beaumaris

Marine World

Cefni
Resr.

angefni

Talwrn

Rhoscefnhir

A5025

Llansadwrn

Childhood

Beaumaris
Courthouse

Llandegfan

A545

MENAI

Lavan Sands
(Traeth Lafan)

Llanfairfechan

15

Rhostrenwfa

3

A5114

B5420

Penmynydd

(AFON

A55

Nant
y-felin

A5

3

Pili Palas
Alms Houses

Menai Bridge
(Porthaethwy)

Upper
Bangor

3 A5

Industrial
Railway NT
Penrhyn
Castle NT

14

13 **15**

Abergwyngregyn

7

Llanfair Pwllgwyngyll

7 a 3

8

Menai
Br

Llandegai

12

A55

Coedydd Aber
Falls

Pentre Berw

Gaerwen

A5

8 a

Britannia
Bri

S

Moel Wnion

Llyn
Anafon

Bryn Celli Ddu
Burial Chamber

Nelson
Statue

9

**Penrhos
Garnedd**

BANGOR
SEE PAGE 82

Tal-y-bont

Cochwillan
Old
Hall

Llanllechid

Aber Falls

NT

Llanddaniel Fab

B4419

Vaynol

NT
Plas

A

10

A4087

BANGOR

11

Rachub

B

2484
Drosgl

3091

FOEL-M

Llangaffo

Castell
Bryn
Gwyn

Caer Leb
Earthwork

A4080

Plas
Coch

A487

Y Felinheli
(Port Dinorwig)

B4547

Glasinfryn

Green
Wood
Cen.

Pentir

A4244

Tregarth

Bryn
Eglwys

Gerlan

Bethesda

Bodowyr Burial
Chamber

Brynsiencyn

Sea
Zoo

250

Saron

Llanddeiniolen

Mynydd

Braichmelyn

wyran

16

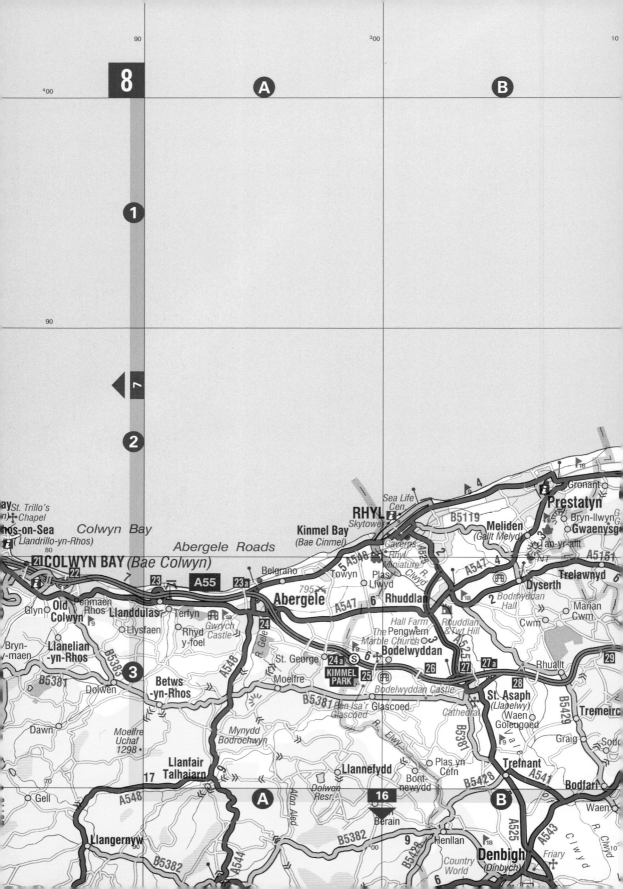

LIVERPOOL

BAY

Crosby Channel

Hightown

Ince Blundell

MAG

Homer Green

Little Thornton

Lunt Se

Great Crosby Hill

Neth Buckl

CROSBY

LITHERLAND

Waterloo

Orrell

Seaforth

BOOTLE

Fort

New Brighton

WALLASEY

Liscard

Egremont

Seacombe

Queensway

Mersey Tunnel

TOLL (Kingsway)

Toxteth

Eve

Leasowe

Bidston

Moreton

Meols

A553

Upton

Claughton

BIRKENHEAD

Red Rocks Marsh

Hilbre Islands Bird Sanctuary

Hilbre Islands

HOYLAKE

Newton

Greasby

Frankby

Woodchurch

Oxton

Prenton

Tranmere

Rock Ferry

Pleas Islar

West Kirby

Grange

Arrowe

B5140

Irby

Thingwall

M53

New Ferry

Caldy

Pensby

Barnston

BEBINGTON

Port Sunlight

Thurstaston

Heswall

Brimstage

Spital

Visitor Centre

Thornton Hough

Brookhurst

Point of Ayr

Talacre

Llawndy

Gayton

Raby

Windle Hill

Willaston

The Wirral

Gayton Sands

Parkgate

B5135

NESTON

Little Neston

Ness Botanic Garden

DANGER AREA

ENGLAND

WALES

Burton

A550

Puddington

Shotwick Hall

Shotwick

Gwespyr

Picton

Pen-y-Fford

Flynnongroyw

Golden Castle

Llanasa

Trelogan

Mostyn

Glan-y-don

Berthengam

Maen Achwyfaen Cross

Rhewl-Mostyn

Whitford (Chwitffordd)

A548

Lloc

A5026

Pant y Wacco

Gorsedd

Greenfield (Maes-glas)

Basingwerk Abbey

Holywell Bank

Whelston

A55

Carmel

Pantasaph

Holywell (Treffynnon)

Bagillt

Puddington

A548

Garden City

Saugha

A5

A494

Sealand

Queensferry

Mancot

Sandyford

Caerwys

FLINTSHIRE

Brynford

Babell

Dolphin

Basingwerk Castle

Flint

Flint (Y Fflint)

Oakenholt

Kelsterton

CONNAH'S QUAY

Shotton

Higher Shotton

Pen-y-cefn

Afon-wen

Ddol

Ysceifiog

Lixwm

Pentre Halkyn

Halkyn (Helygain)

Tirnewydd

964

Halkyn Mountains

Flint Mountain

Northop Hall

Fwloe

Ewloe

CLWYDIAN RANGE

Moel Famau

Rhoesmor

Wat's Dyke

Northop

B5126

B5125

Shotton

Soughton (Sychdyn)

Alltami

Aston

Hawarden

Rhydymwyn

Llangwyfan

Moel Famau

Liverpool to Dublin 7hrs. 30mins.

Liverpool to:
Douglas 4hrs. (Seasonal)
Douglas 2hrs. 30mins. (Fast Ferry, Seasonal)
Dublin 4hrs. (Fast Ferry)

Birkenhead to:
Belfast 8hrs.

Mostyn to Dublin 6hrs.

Liverpool to Dublin 7hrs. 30mins.

Liverpool to:
Douglas 4hrs. (Seasonal)
Douglas 2hrs. 30mins.
(Fast Ferry, Seasonal)
Dublin 4hrs. (Fast Ferry)

Birkenhead to:
Belfast 8hrs.

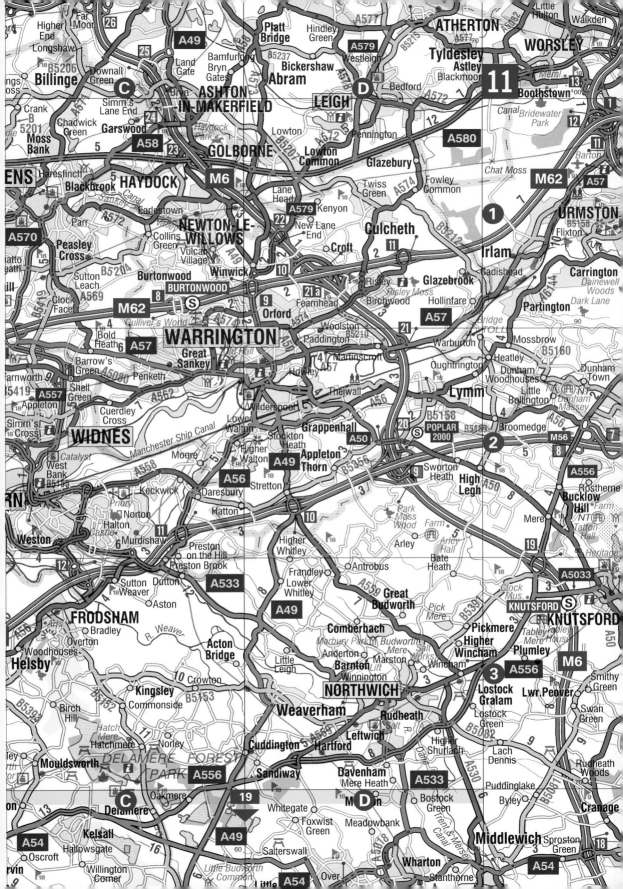

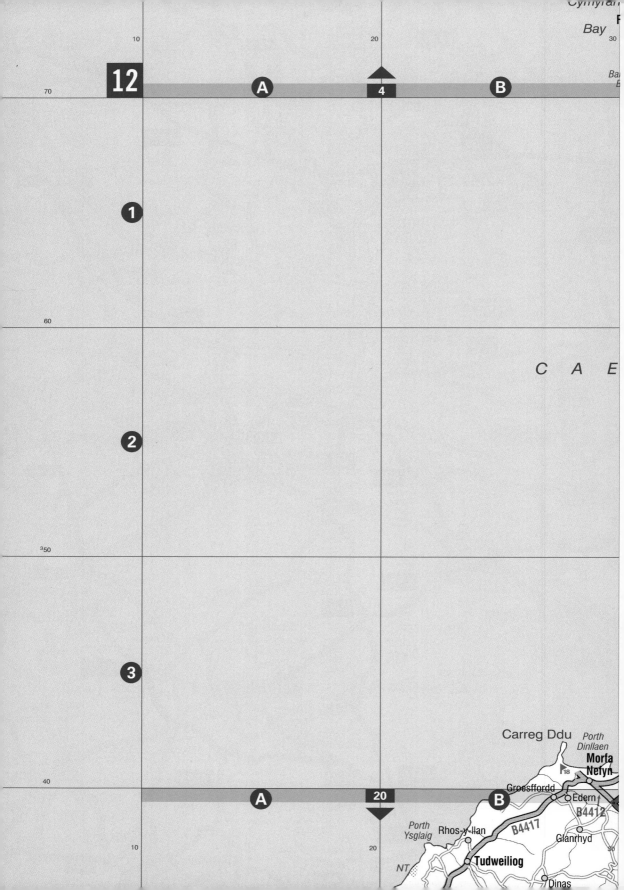

A   4   B

10   20   Bay   30

70

1

60

C A E

2

³50

3

Carreg Ddu   *Porth Dinllaen*

Morfa Nefyn

Groesffordd

A   20   B   Edern

40

Porth Ysglaig   Rhos-y-llan   B4417   Glanrhyd

10   20   30

NT   **Tudweiliog**

Dinas

B4412

Cymyran   Bay

18

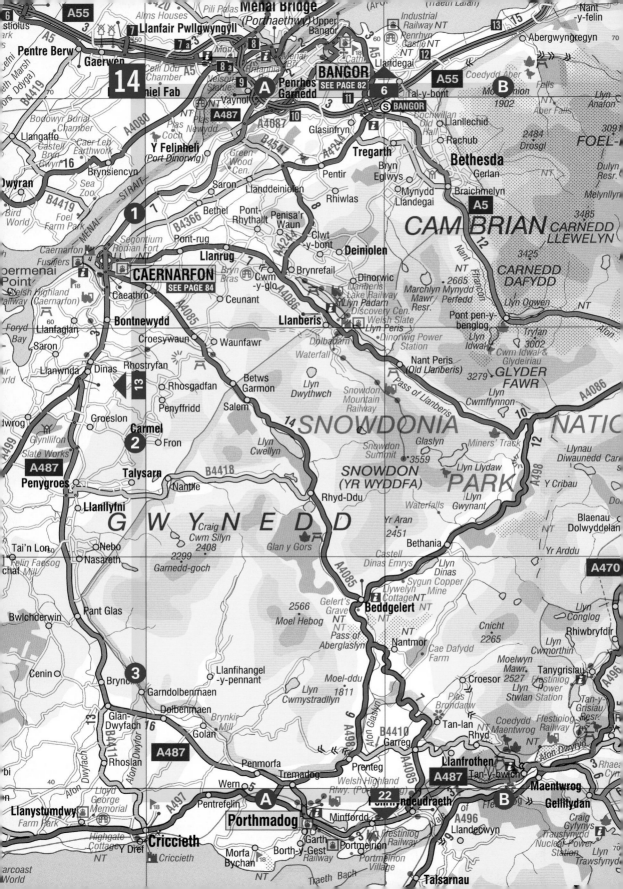

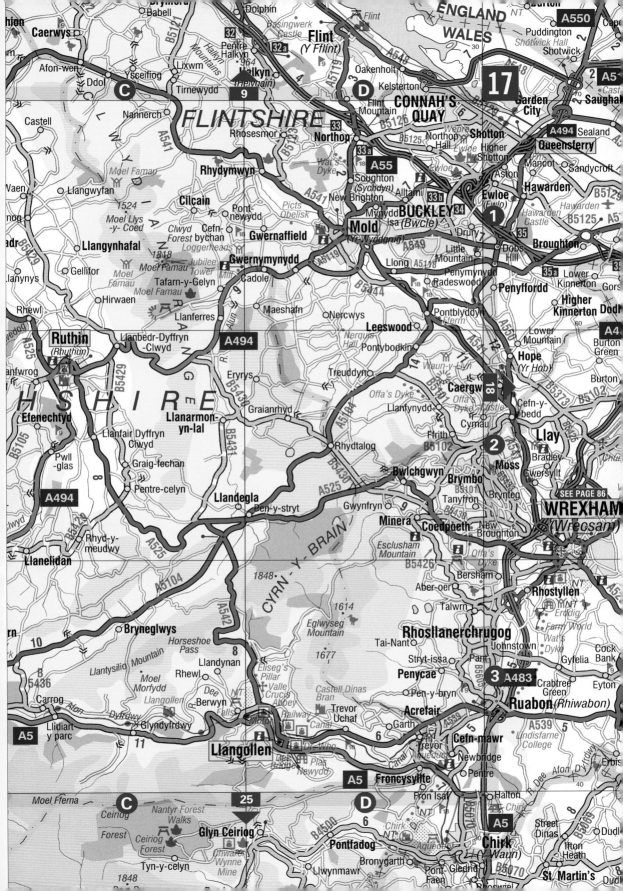

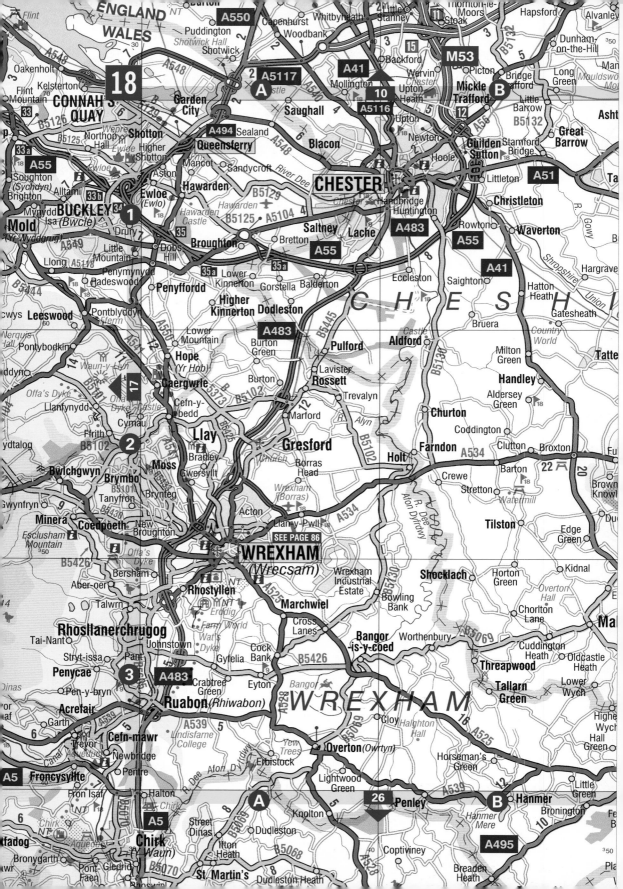

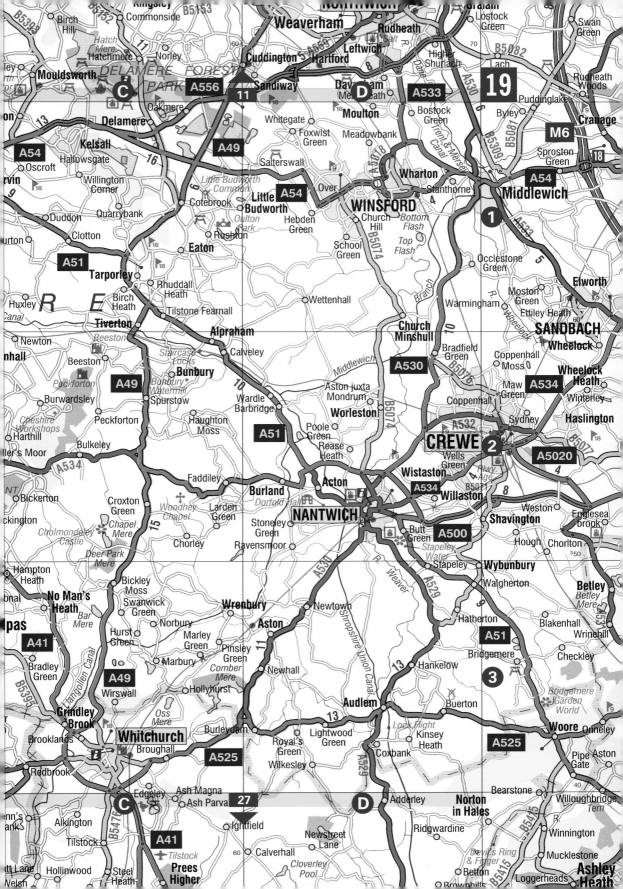

Carreg Ddu
Porth Dinllaen
Morfa Nefyn

A

12

B

Groesffordd
Edern
B4412

Porth Ysglaig
Rhos-y-llan
Glanrhyd

NT
Tudweiliog
Dinas

Porth Colmon
Rhos-ddu
•Fort
Garn-fadryn

Penllech
Llaniestyn

Llangwnnadl
Bryn-mawr

Pen-y-graig

Penrhyn Mawr
Sarn Meyllteyrn

Bryncroes

L L
Botwnnog
16
B4413

Rhydllos

Porth Oer
Rhoshirwaun
NT
NT

NT
Llan

NT
Llawr Dref

Braich Anelog
Penycaerau
Rhiw
Llanengan

Anelog
NT
Plas-yn-Rhiw
Bwlchto

NT
Llanfaelrhys
NT
Porth Neigwl or Hell's Mouth

Braich y Pwll
NT

2
Uwchmynydd
Aberdaron Bay
Ynys Gwylan-fawr
NT
Trwyn Cilan

Aberdaron
NT

BARDSEY SOUND (SWNT ENLLI)
Pen y Cil

St. Mary's Abbey

Bardsey Island (Ynys Enlli)

C A

(B

3

A
B

210
20
30

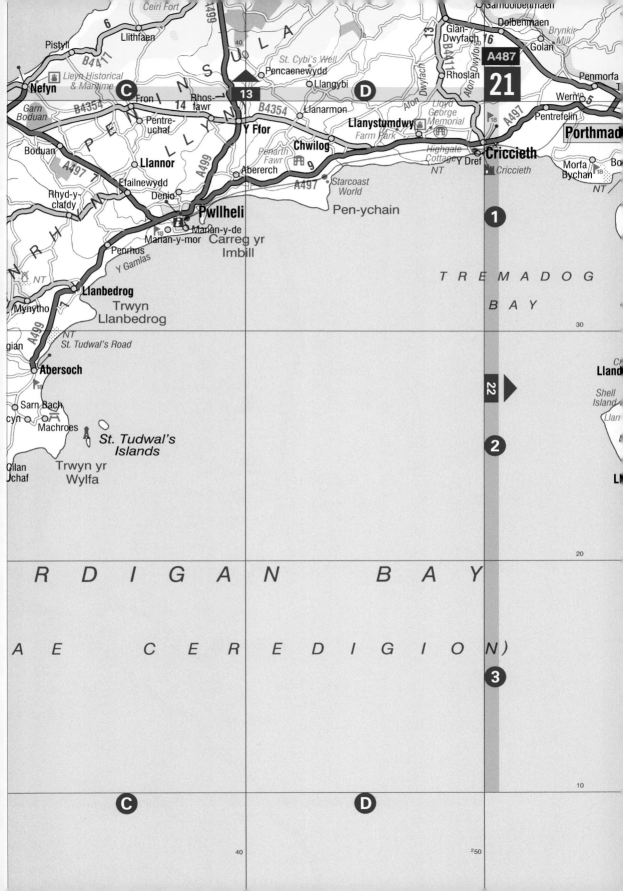

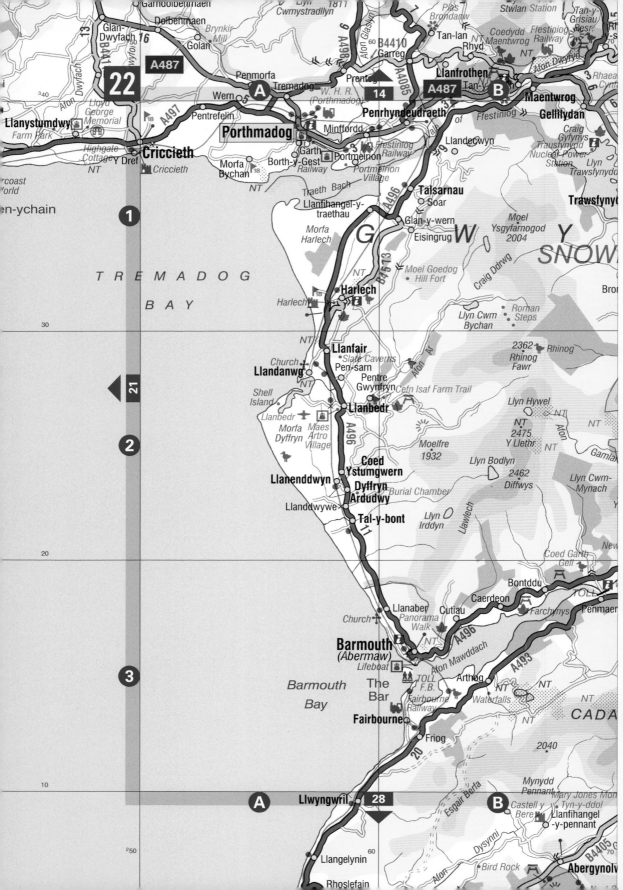

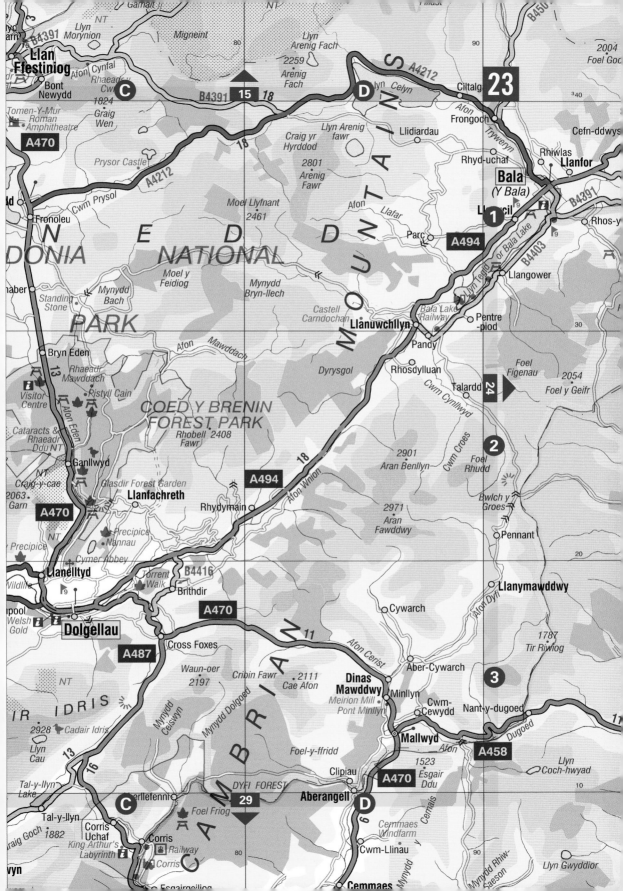

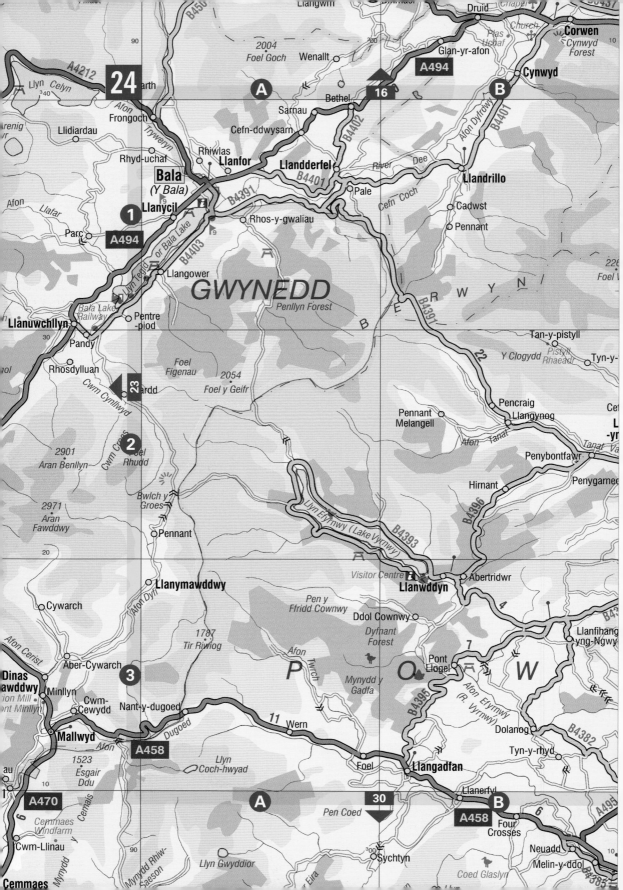

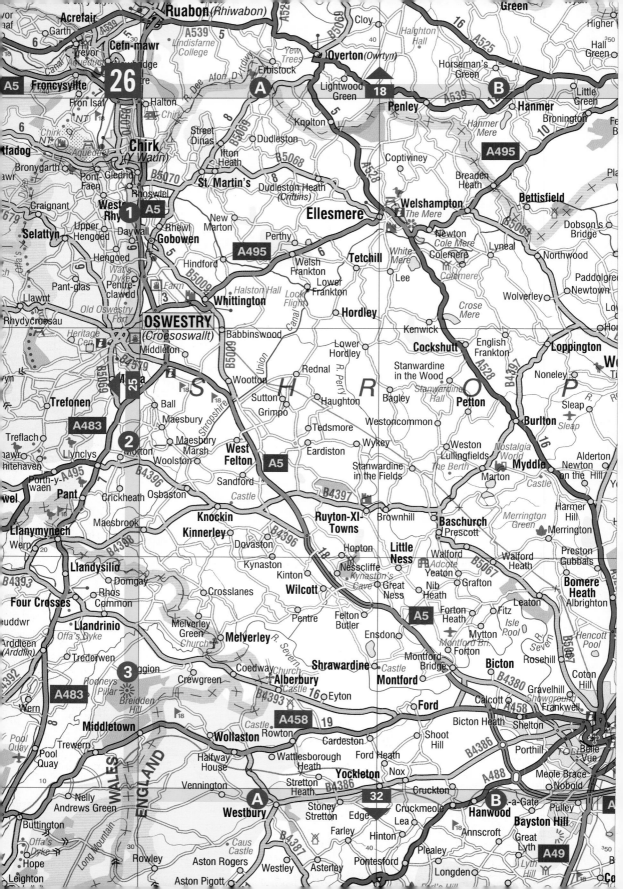

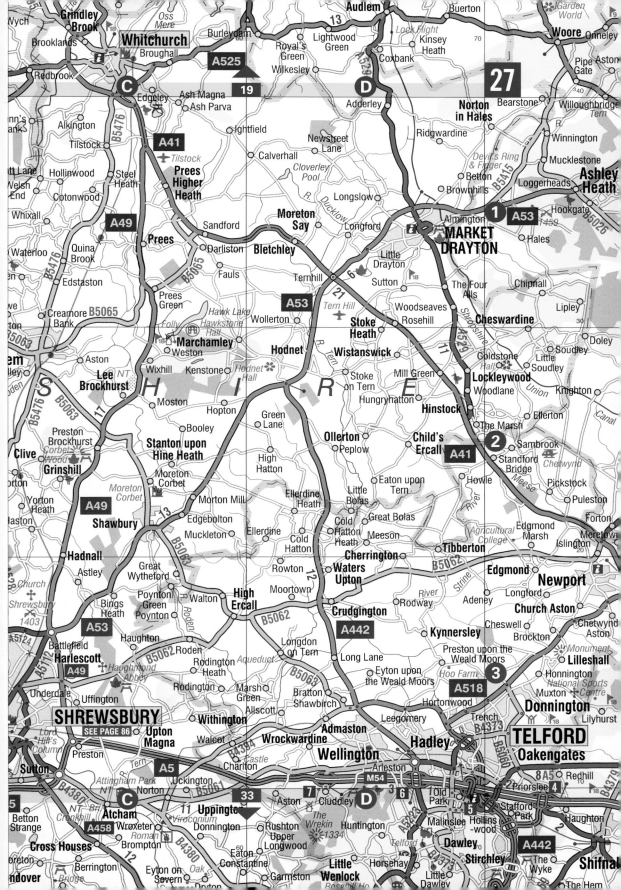

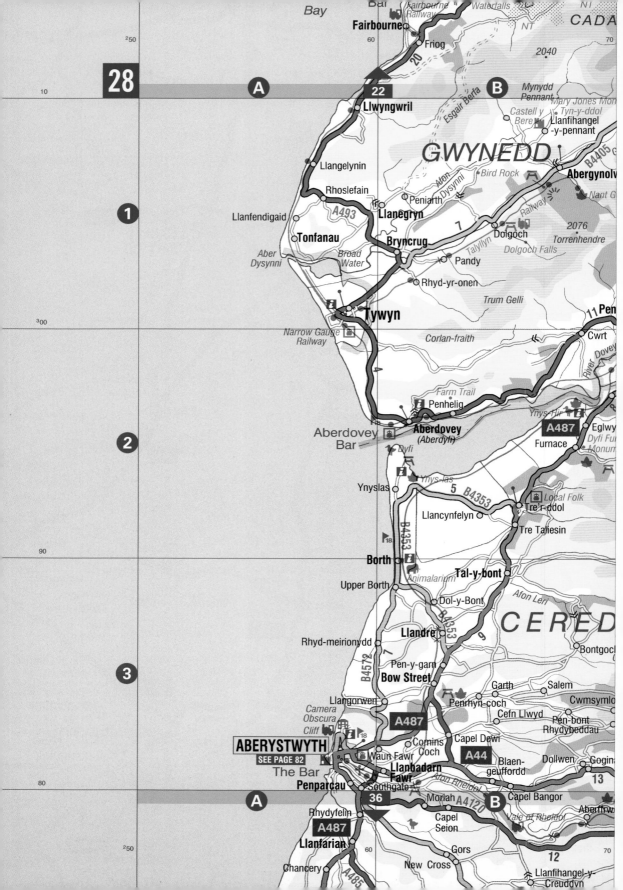

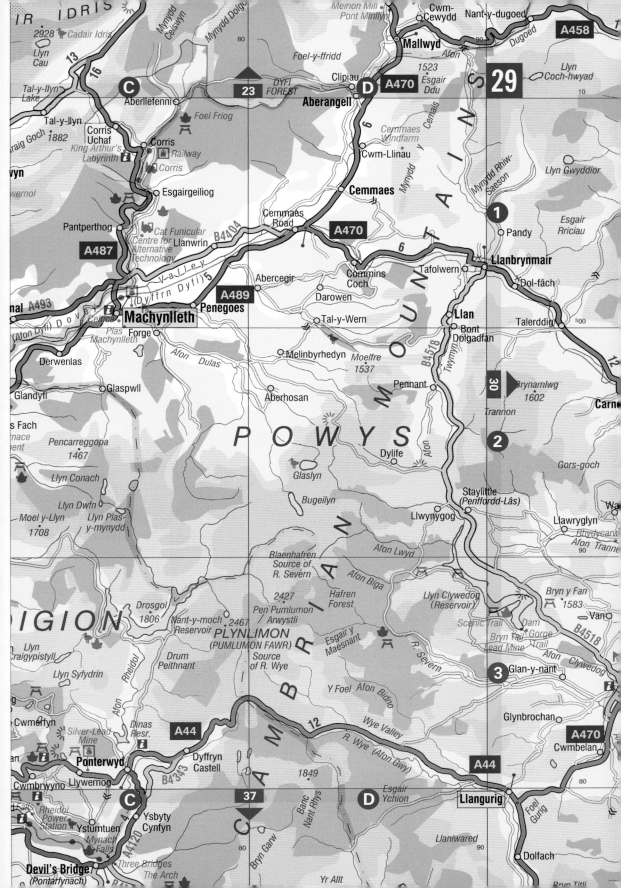

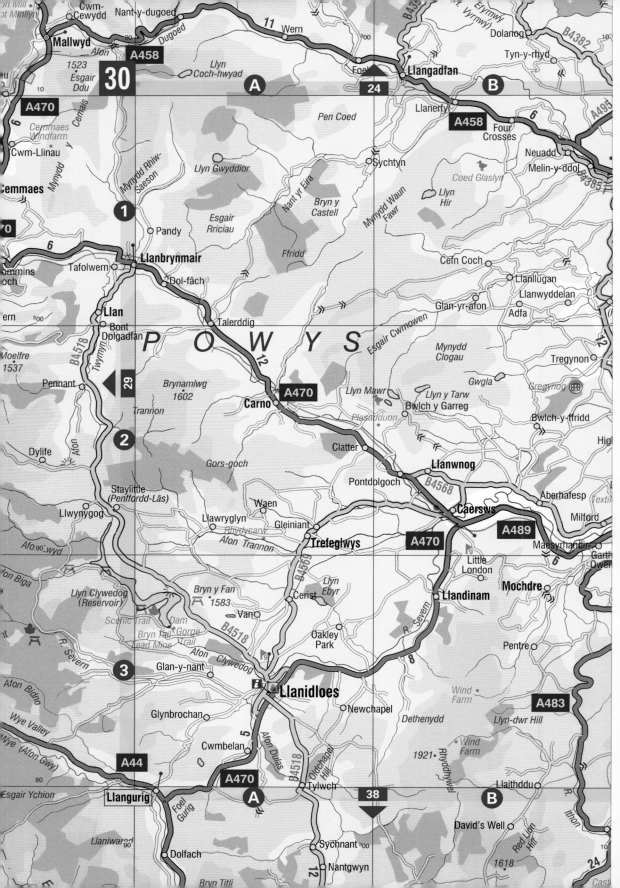

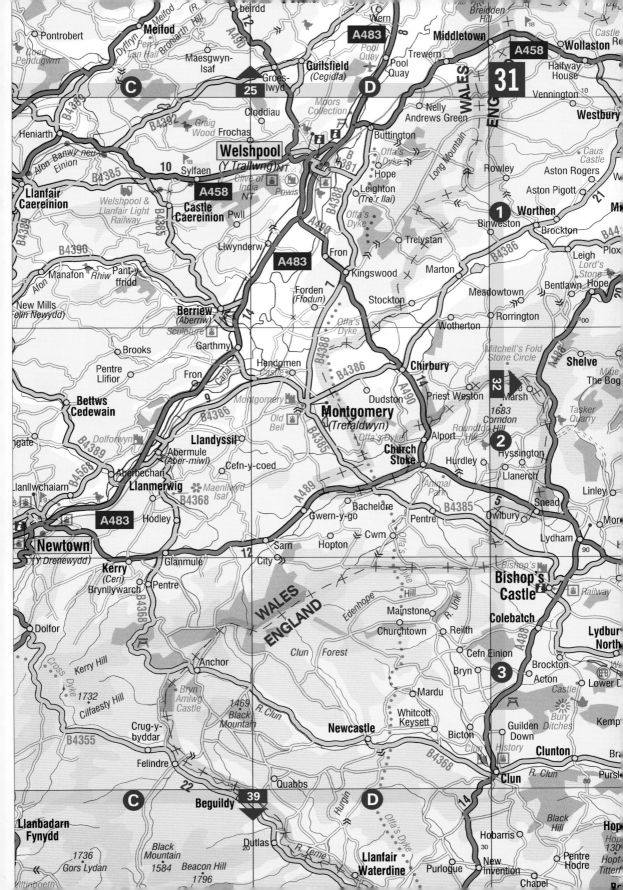

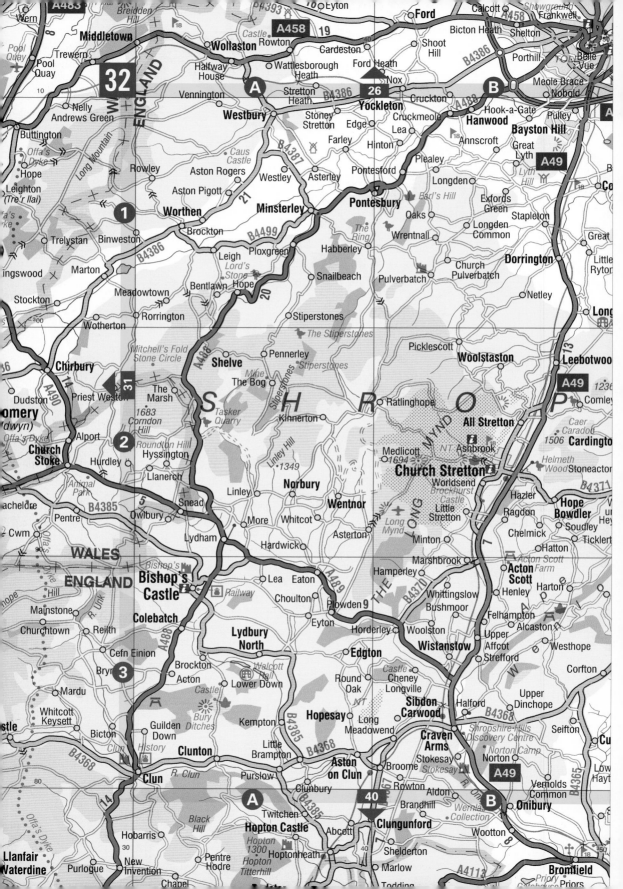

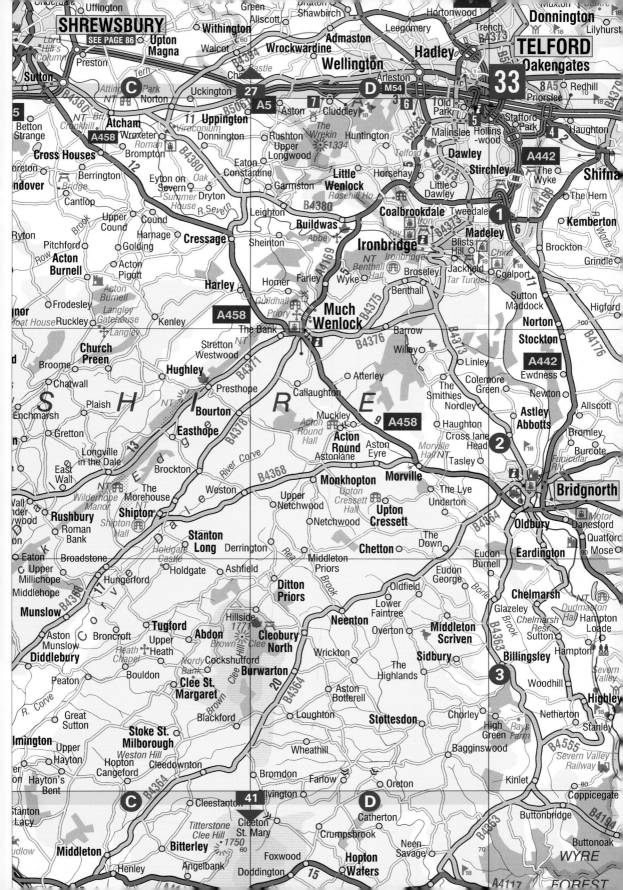

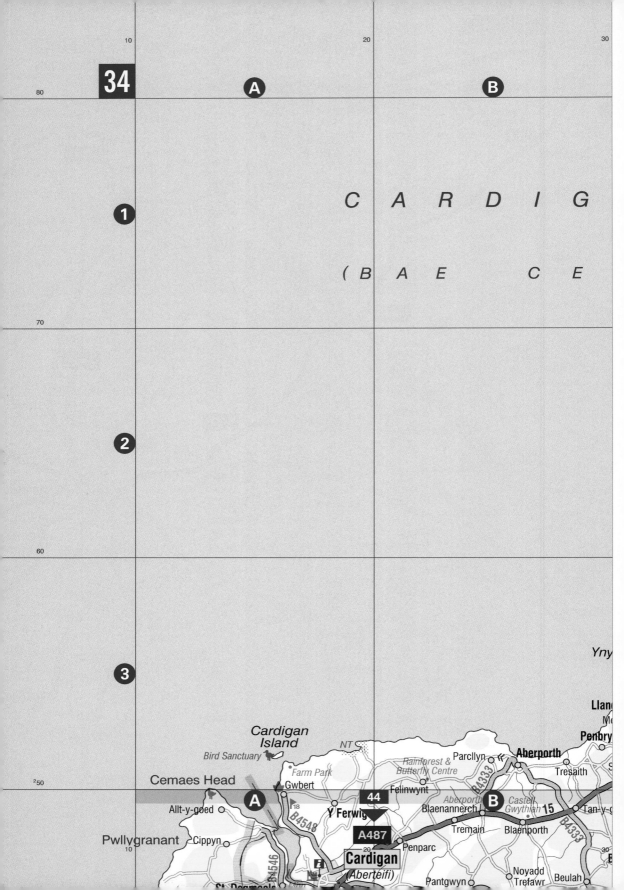

10　　　　　　　　　20　　　　　　　　　30

80

Ⓐ　　　　　　　　　Ⓑ

❶

C A R D I G

(B A E　　　C E

70

❷

60

❸

Yny

Llan

Mo

Penbry

Cardigan Island
Bird Sanctuary

NT

Rainforest &
Butterfly Centre

Parcllyn　《《　**Aberporth**

Tresaith

S

Farm Park

Gwbert

²50

Cemaes Head

Ⓐ

18

B4548

Felinwynt

Aberporth

Ⓑ　Castell
Gwythian

15

B4333

Allt-y-goed

44

Y Ferwig

Blaenannerch

Tan-y-

A487

Tremain

Blaenporth

Pwllygranant　Cippyn

10

20　Penparc

Cardigan
(Aberteifi)

Pantgwyn

Noyadd
Trefawr

Beulah

B4546

St Dogmaels

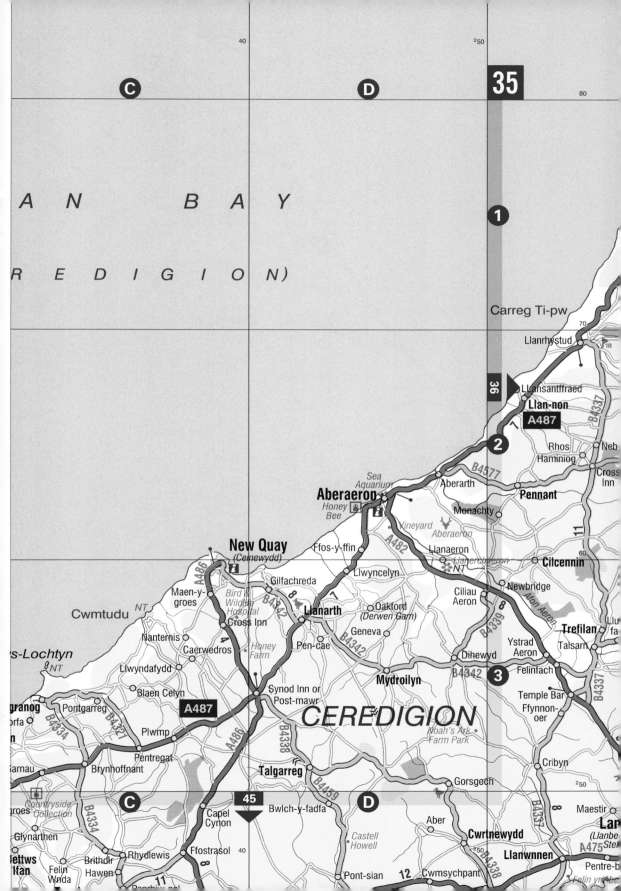

40   250   80

1

CARDIGAN BAY

(CEREDIGION)

Carreg Ti-pw

70

Llanrhystud   18

36   LLansantffraed

Llan-non   B4337

A487

7

2   Rhos
Haminiog   Neb

Sea
Aquarium   Aberarth   B4577   Cross
Inn

Aberaeron   **Pennant**

Honey
Bee

Monachty

Vineyard
Aberaeron   11

Llanaeron

New Quay   *Ffos-y-ffin*   A482   Llanaeron
(Ceinewydd)   NT   **Cilcennin**   60

Llwyncelyn   Llanerchaeron
NT

Maen-y-   Bird &   Gilfachreda   Ciliau   Newbridge
groes   Wildlife   8   Aeron
Hospital   7

Cwmtudu   NT   **Llanarth**   Oakford   B4339   8   **Trefilan**
Cross Inn   (Derwen Gam)   Llu
fa
Nanternis   Honey   Geneva   B4342   Ystrad   Talsarn
Caerwedros   Farm   Pen-cae   Aeron
s-Lochtyn   4   Dihewyd   Felinfach   **3**
NT   Llwyndafydd   B4342

Blaen Celyn   Synod Inn or   **Mydroilyn**   Temple Bar
Pontgarreg   Post-mawr   Ffynnon-
granog   **A487**   oer
rfa   B4327   A486   **CEREDIGION**   Cribyn
Plwmp   B4338   Noah's Ark
arnau   Pentregat   Farm Park   250

Brynhoffnant   **Talgarreg**   **Gorsgoch**   Maestir

45   B4459   B4337   8

Countryside   **C**   Capel   Bwlch-y-fadfa   **D**   Aber   **Lar**
Collection   Cynon   Castell   (Llanbe
roes   40   Howell   **Cwrtnewydd**   A475   Ste

B4334   8   **Llanwnnen**   Pentre-b
Glynarthen   250
ettws   Brithdir   Rhydlewis   Ffostrasol   Pont-sian   12   Cwmsychpant   Felin yr
Ifan   Felin   Hawen   11   B4338
Wnda

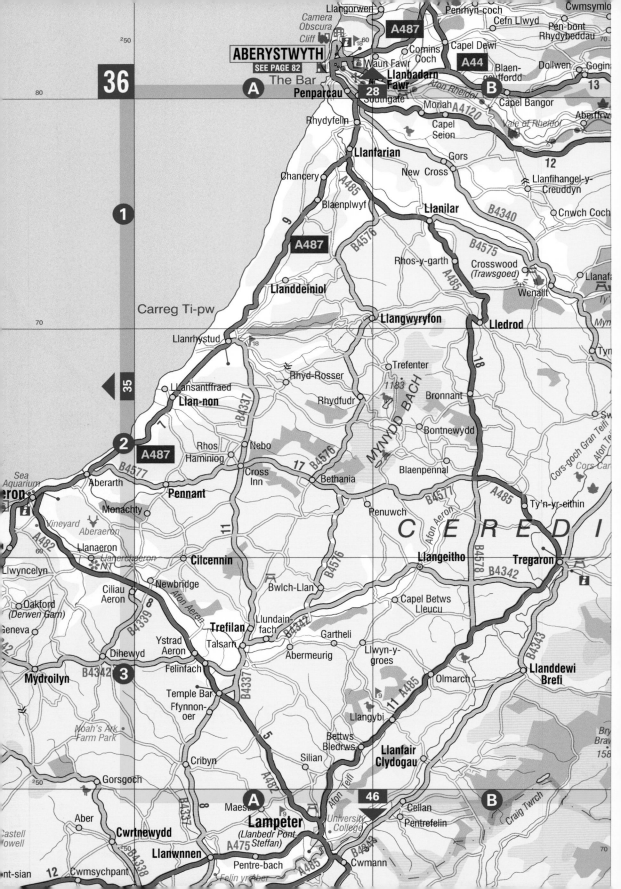

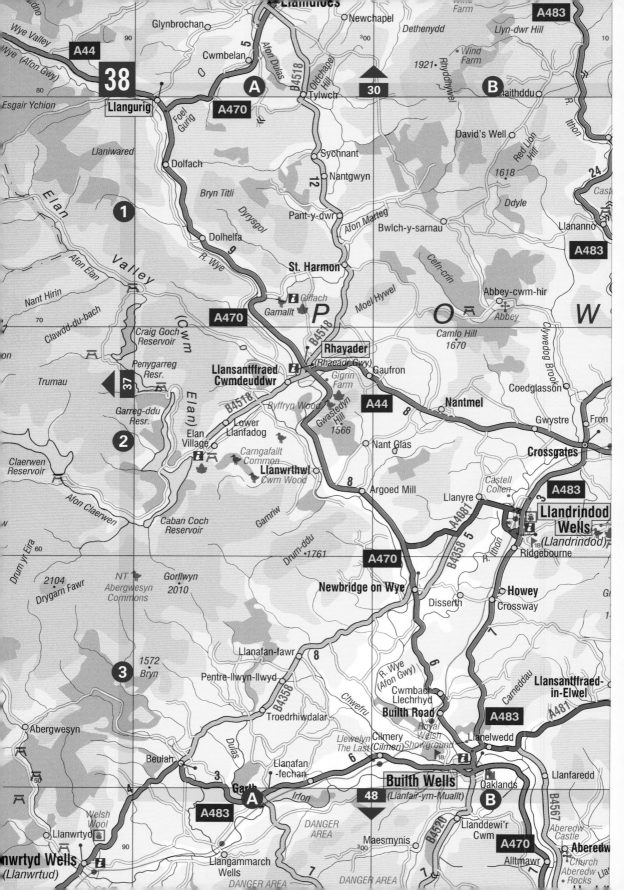

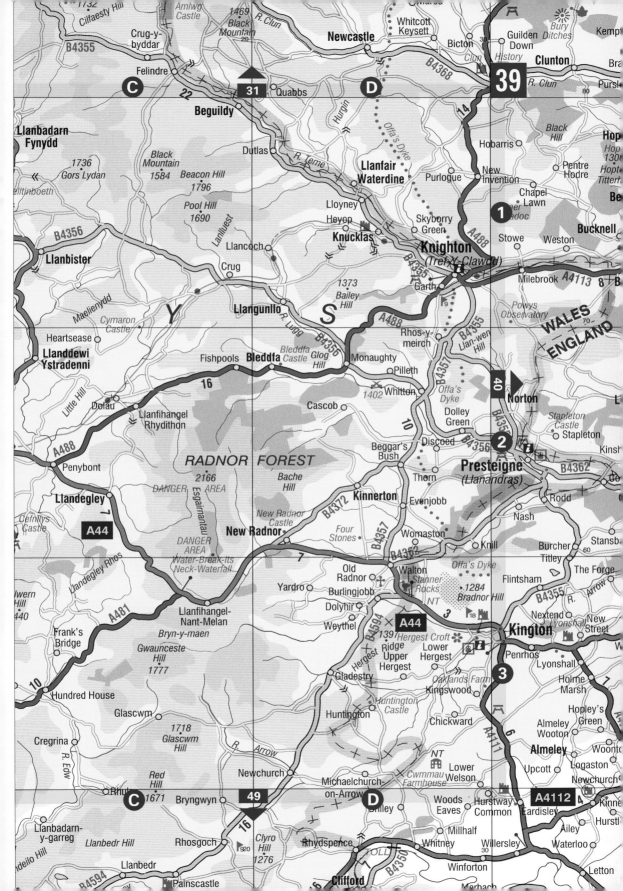

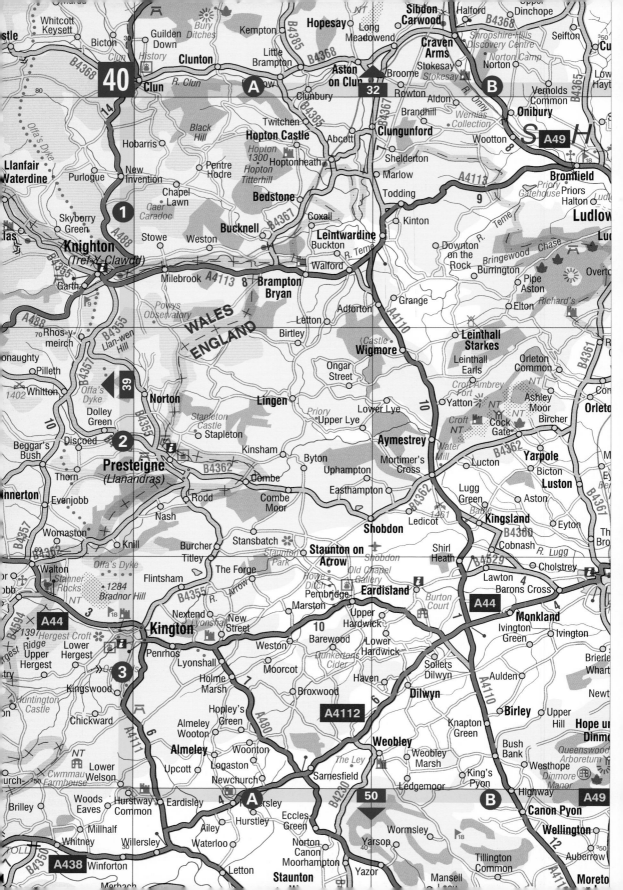

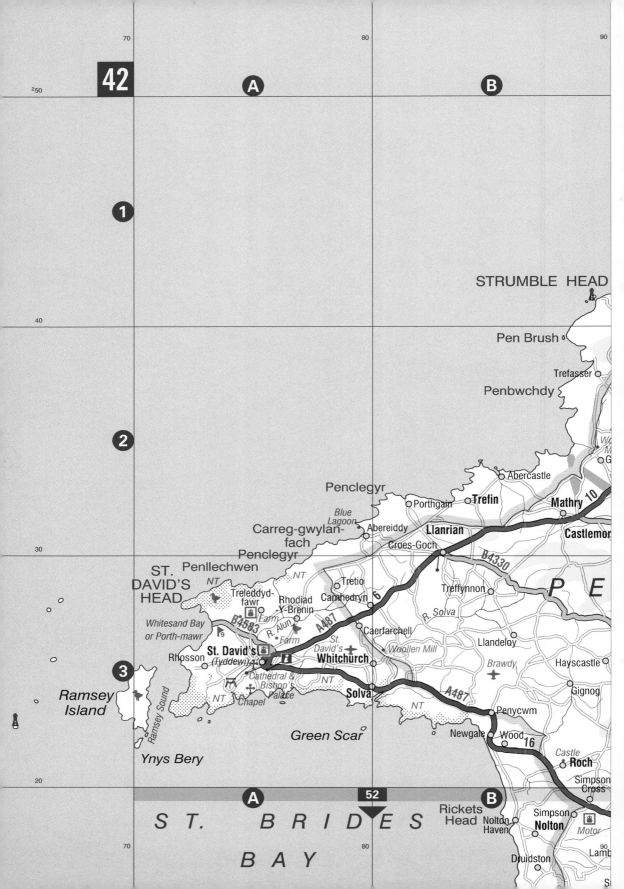

42

A

B

1

STRUMBLE HEAD

40

Pen Brush

Trefasser

Penbwchdy

2

Penclegyr

Abercastle

Blue Lagoon

Porthgain

Trefin

Mathry 10

Carreg-gwylan-fach

Abereiddy

Llanrian

Castlemor

30

Penclegyr

Croes-Goch

B4330

P E

Penllechwen

NT

ST. DAVID'S HEAD

NT

Treleddyd-fawr

Tretio

Cathedryn

6

Treffynnon

Rhodiad-Y-Brenin

A487

B4583

R. Solva

Whitesand Bay or Porth-mawr

R. Alun

Caerfarchell

Llandeloy

Farm

St. David's

Hayscastle

Rhosson

St. David's
(Tyddewi)

Whitchurch

Woollen Mill

Brawdy

Gignog

3

Cathedral & Bishop's Palace

NT

Ramsey Island

Chapel

NT

Solva

A487

Castle

Hayscastle

Ramsey Sound

Roch

Penycwm

Green Scar

16

Newgale

Wood

Ynys Bery

Simpson Cross

20

A

52

B

Rickets Head

Simpson

S T.   B R I D E S

Nolton Haven

Nolton

Motor

B A Y

Druidston

Lamb

S

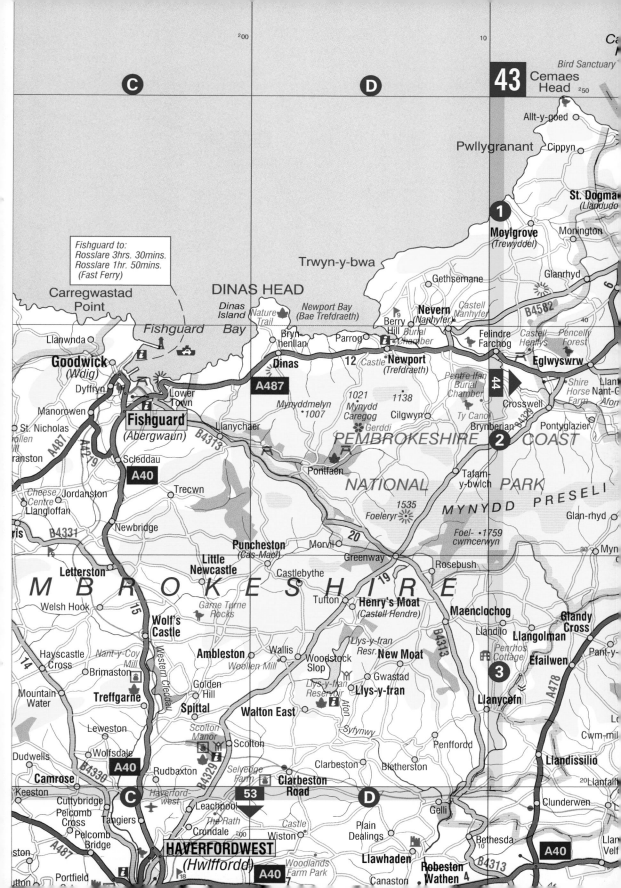

C

D

Bird Sanctuary

Cemaes Head 250

Allt-y-goed

Pwllygranant

Cippyn

St. Dogma (Llandudo)

1

Moylgrove (Trewyddel)

Monington

Glanrhyd

Gethsemane

Trwyn-y-bwa

B4582

Castell Nanhyfer

Nevern (Nanhyfer)

Glan-rhyd

40

Fishguard to:
Rosslare 3hrs. 30mins.
Rosslare 1hr. 50mins.
(Fast Ferry)

Carregwastad Point

DINAS HEAD

Newport Bay (Bae Trefdraeth)

Berry Hill

Felindre Farchog

Castell Henllys

Pencelli Forest

Dinas Island

Nature Trail

Burial Chamber

6

Fishguard Bay

Bryn henllan

Parrog

Eglwyswrw

Llan

Llanwnda

Dinas

Newport (Trefdraeth)

Pentre Ifan Burial Chamber

44

Shire Horse Farm

Nant-e Afon

Goodwick (Wdig)

A487

12 Castle

Crosswell

B4330

Dyffryn

Lower Town

Mynyddmelyn 1007

1021 Mynydd Caregog

1138

Cilgwyn

Ty Canol

Brynberian

Pontyglazier

Manorowen

Fishguard (Abergwaun)

Llanychaer

B4313

Gerddi

PEMBROKESHIRE

COAST

St. Nicholas

ollen ranston

A487

B4329

Scleddau

A40

Trecwn

Pontfaen

NATIONAL

Tafarn-y-bwlch

PARK

MYNYDD PRESELI

Cheese Centre

Llangloffan

Jordanston

1535 Foeleryr

Glan-rhyd

ris

B4331

Newbridge

20

Foel- 1759 cwmcerwyn

30 Myn

Morvil

Greenway

Rosebush

Letterston

Puncheston (Cas Mael)

M B R O K E S H I R E

Little Newcastle

Castlebythe

19

Welsh Hook

Game Turne Rocks

Tufton

Henry's Moat (Castell Hendre)

Maenclochog

Glandy Cross

Wolf's Castle

Llandilo

Llangolman

Hayscastle Cross

Nant-y-Coy Mill

Ambleston

Wallis

Llys-y-fran Resr.

New Moat

Penrhos Cottage

Efailwen

Pant-y-

14

Brimaston

Woollen Mill

Woodstock Slop

Gwastad

3

A478

Mountain Water

Golden Hill

Llys-y-fran Reservoir

Llys-y-tran

Llanycefn

Lo

Treffgarne

Spittal

Walton East

Afon Syfynwy

Cwm-mil

Leweston

Penffordd

Llandissilio

Dudwells

Wolfsdale

Scolton Manor

Scolton

Clarbeston

Bletherston

20 Llanfall

Camrose

A40

Rudbaxton

Selvedge Farm

Clarbeston Road

Gelli

Clunderwen

Keeston

Cuttybridge

Haverford-west

53

D

Bethesda

A40

Pelcomb Cross

Leachpool

The Rath

Castle

Plain Dealings

Llan Velf

Pelcomb Bridge

Crundale 200

Wiston

Llawhaden

Robeston Wathen 4

A487

ston

Portfield

18

HAVERFORDWEST (Hwlffordd)

A40

Woodlands Farm Park

Canaston

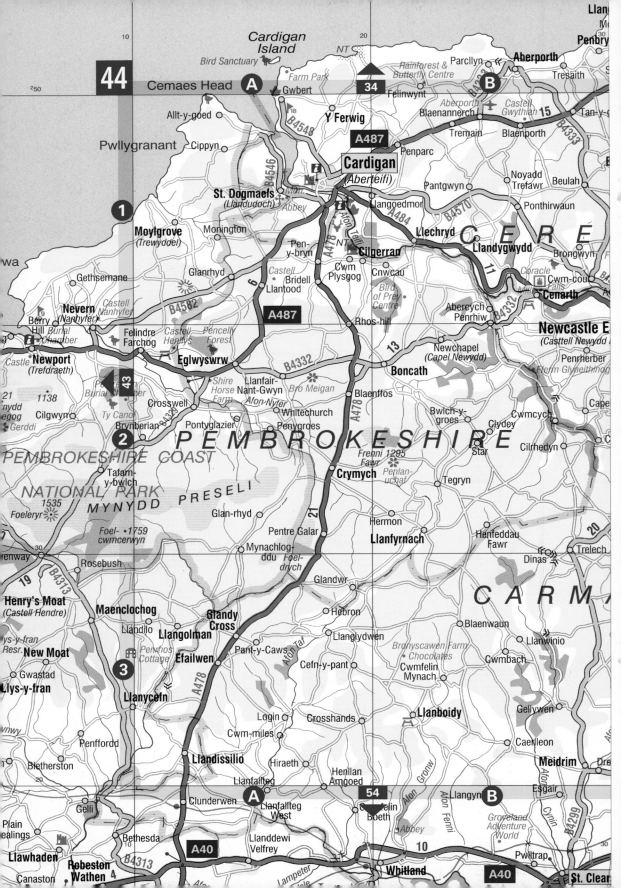

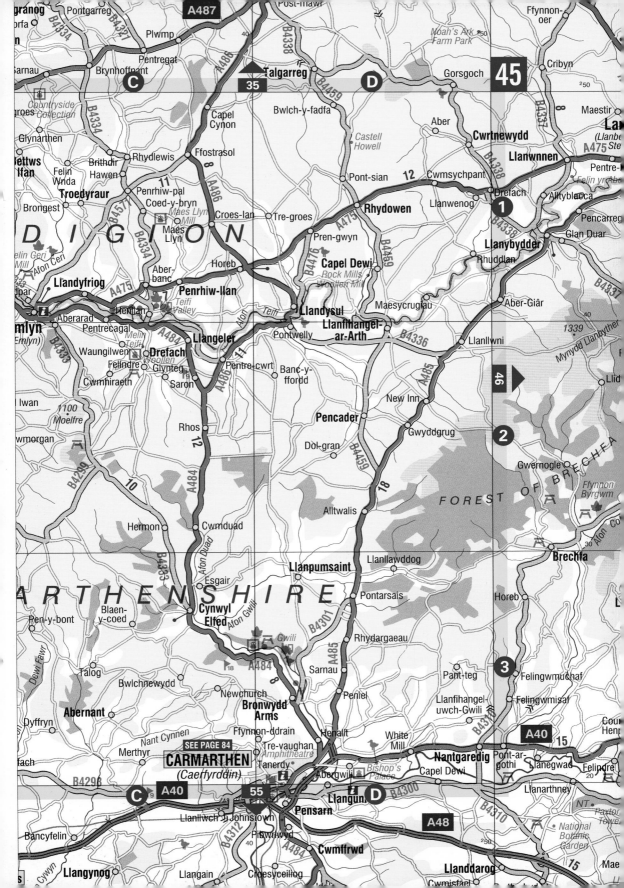

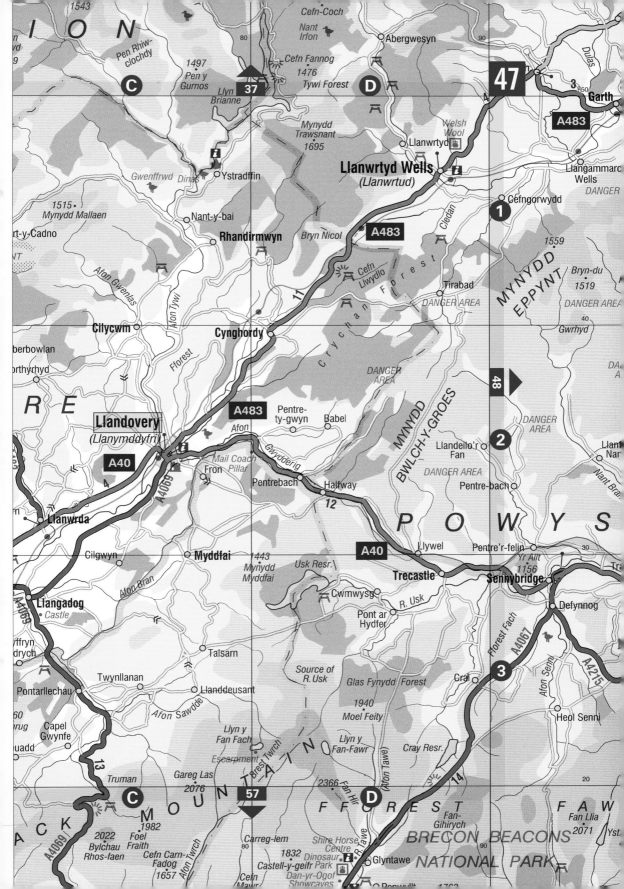

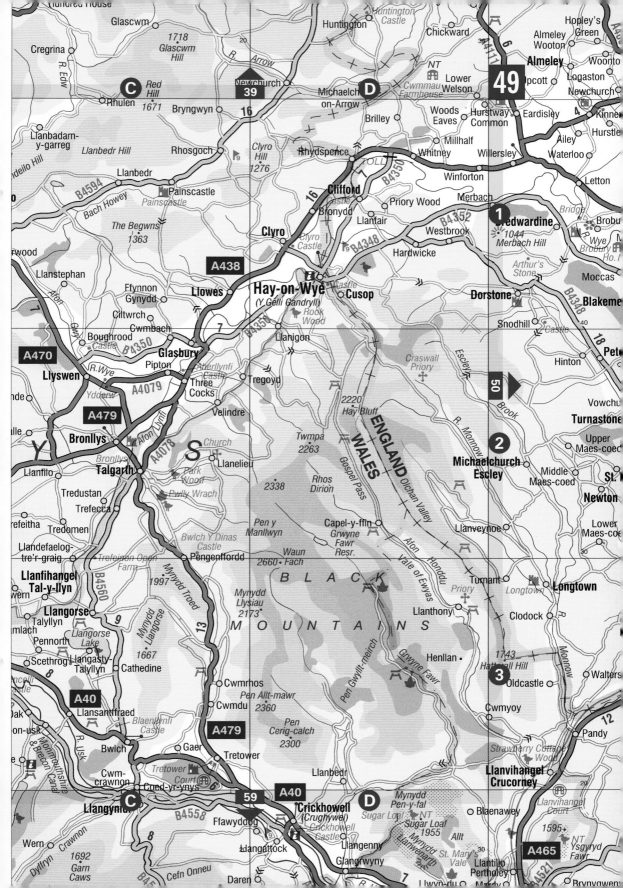

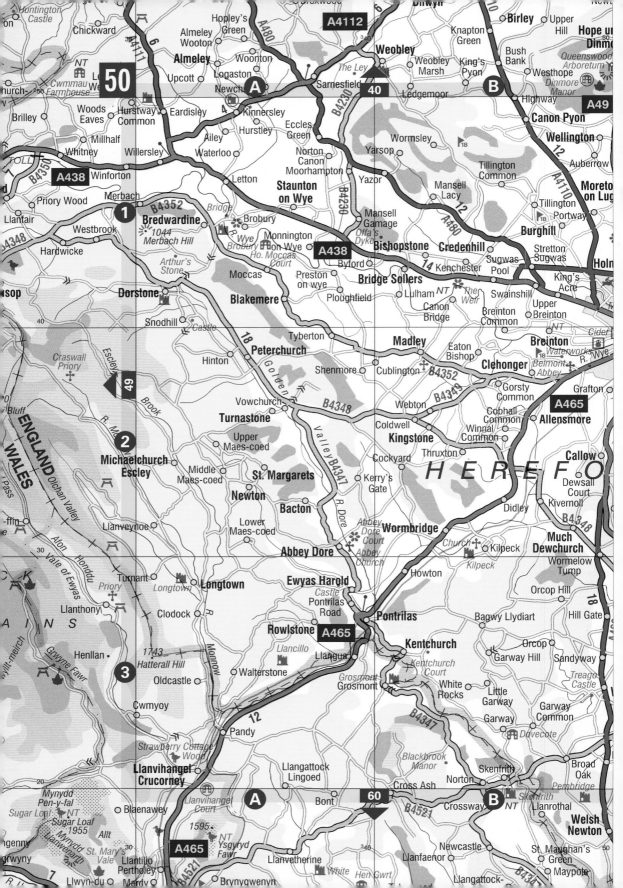

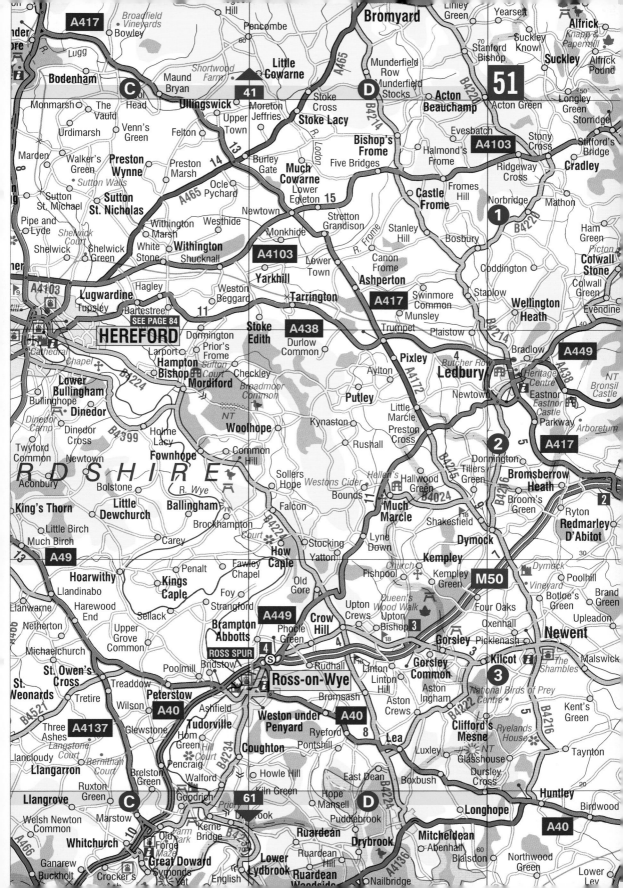

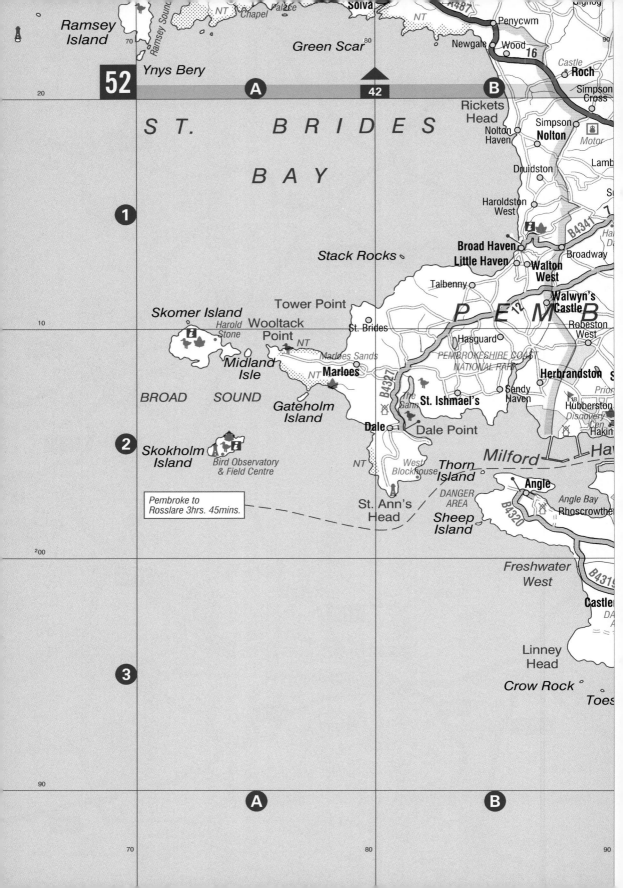

Ramsey Island

Ynys Bery

Green Scar 80

52 A 42 B

S T.   B R I D E S

B A Y

Chapel
Palace
Solva
Penycwm
Newgale
Wood
16
Castle
Roch
Simpson Cross

Rickets Head
Simpson
Nolton Haven
Nolton
Motor
Druidston
Lamb

Haroldston West

20

1

Stack Rocks

Haroldston West
Broad Haven
Little Haven
Walton West
Broadway

10

Talbenny

Walwyn's Castle
Robeston West

Skomer Island
Harold Stone
Wooltack Point
Tower Point
St. Brides
Hasguard

P E M B

PEMBROKESHIRE COAST NATIONAL PARK

Marloes Sands

Midland Isle
Marloes
NT
B4327

Herbrandston
Sandy Haven

BROAD   SOUND

Gateholm Island

St. Ishmael's

Hubberston
Discovery Cen
Hakin

2

Skokholm Island
Bird Observatory & Field Centre

Dale
Dale Point

Milford Ha

NT
West Blockhouse

Thorn Island
Angle
Angle Bay
Rhoscrowthe

Pembroke to Rosslare 3hrs. 45mins.

St. Ann's Head

DANGER AREA

Sheep Island

B4320

200

Freshwater West

B4319

Castle

3

Linney Head

Crow Rock

Toes

90

A B

70 80 90

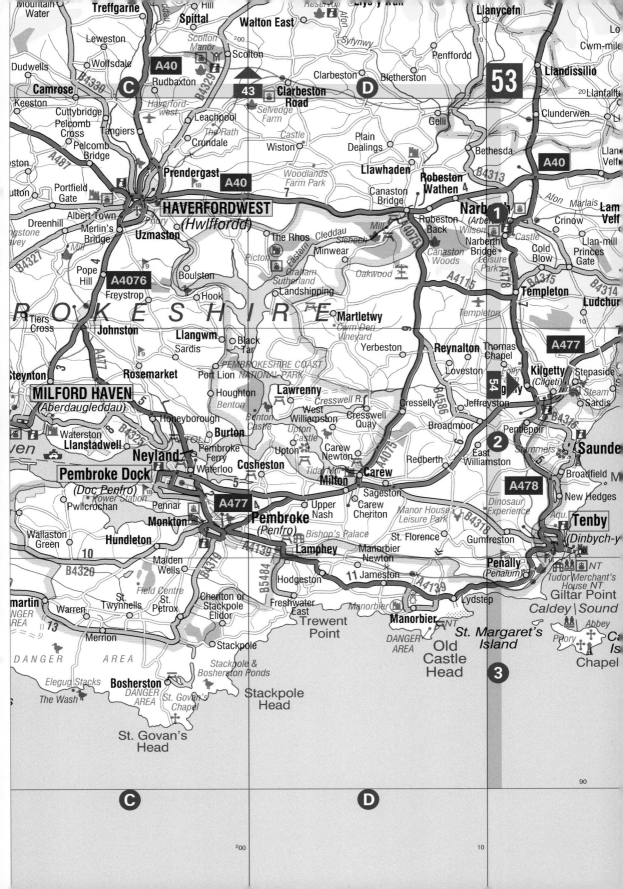

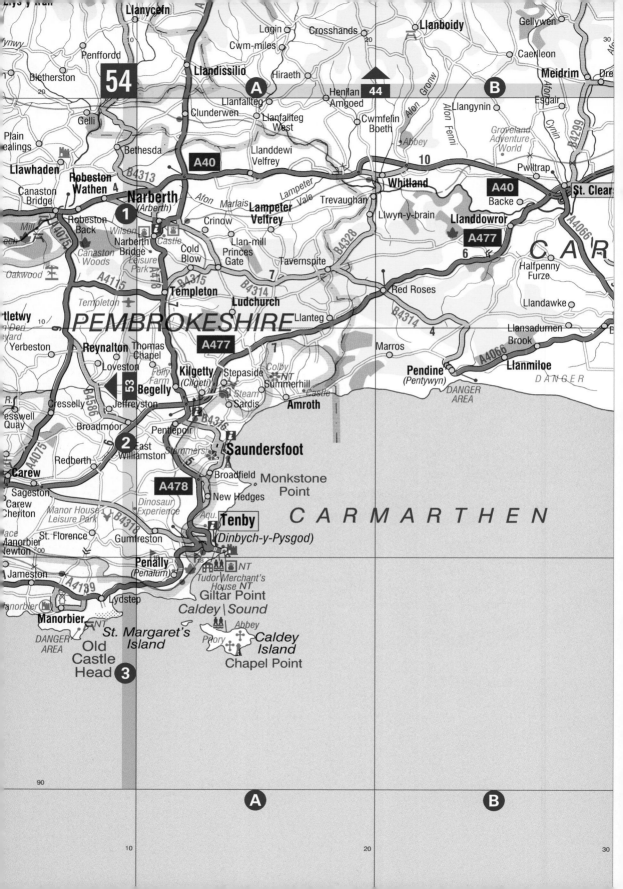

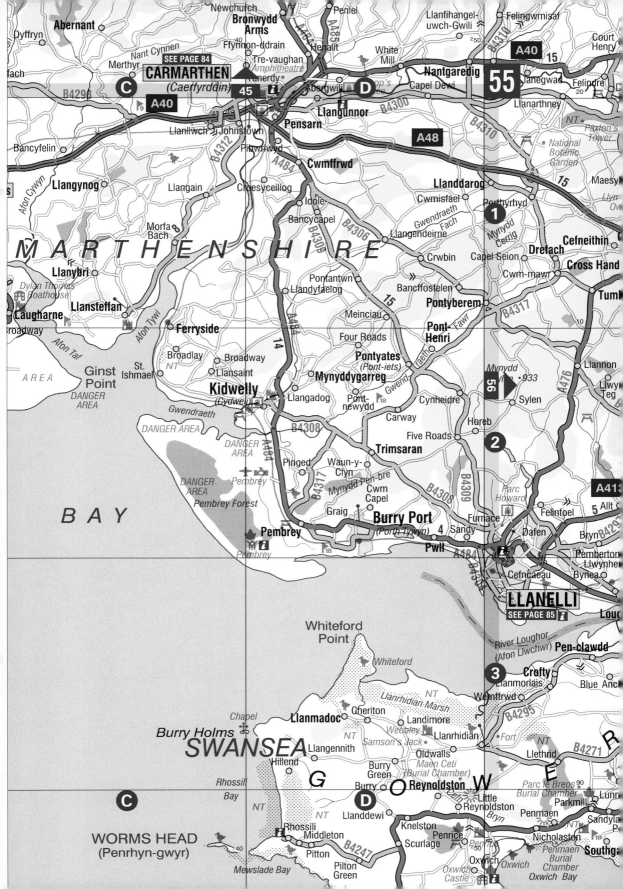

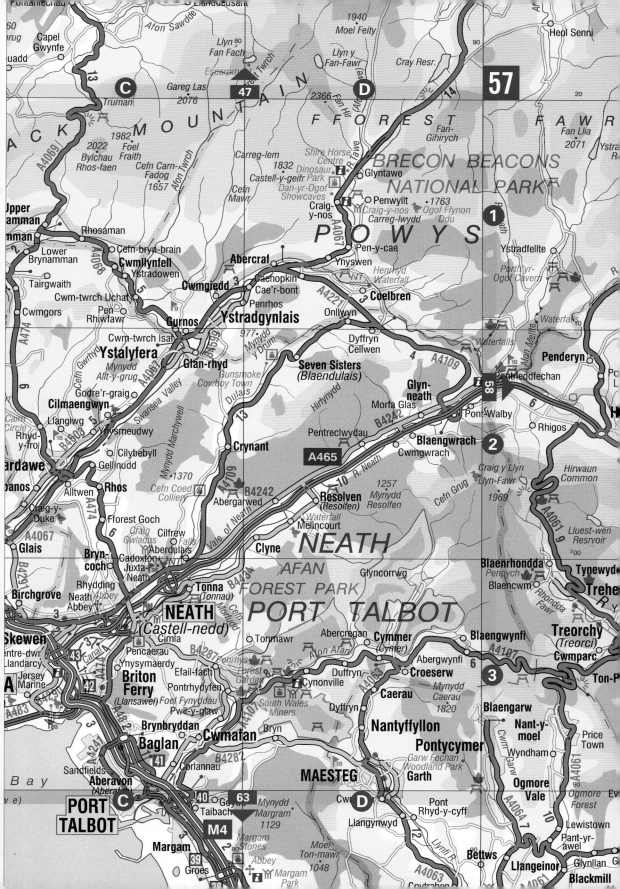

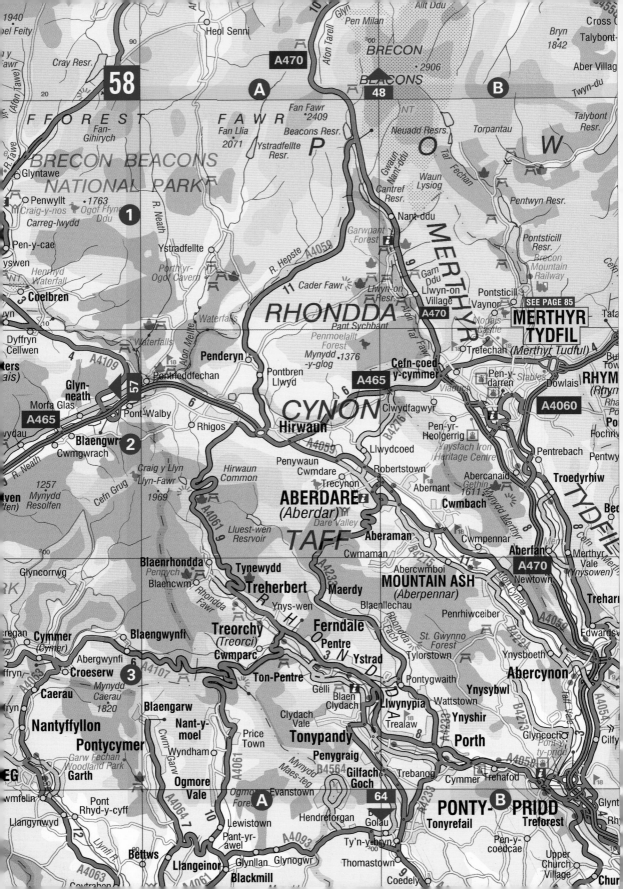

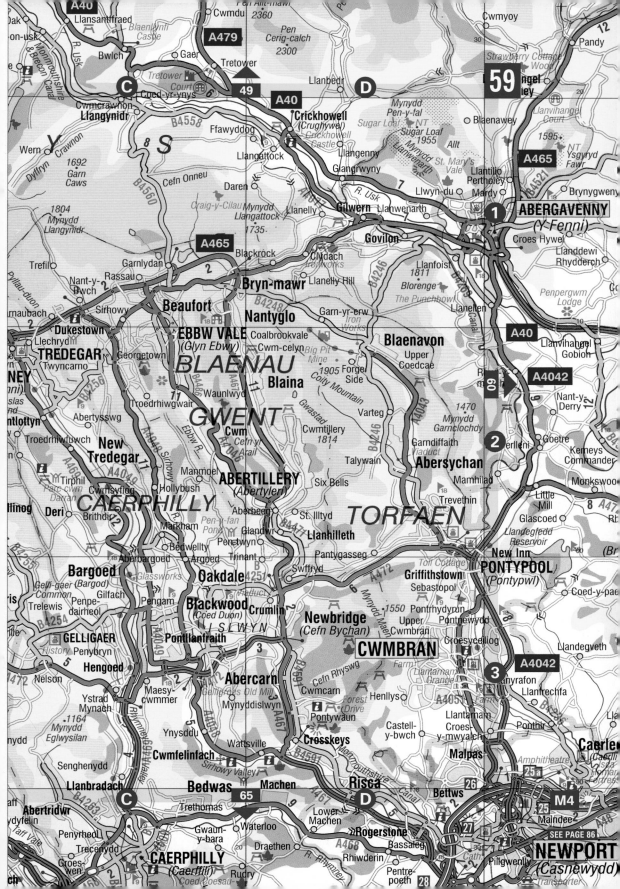

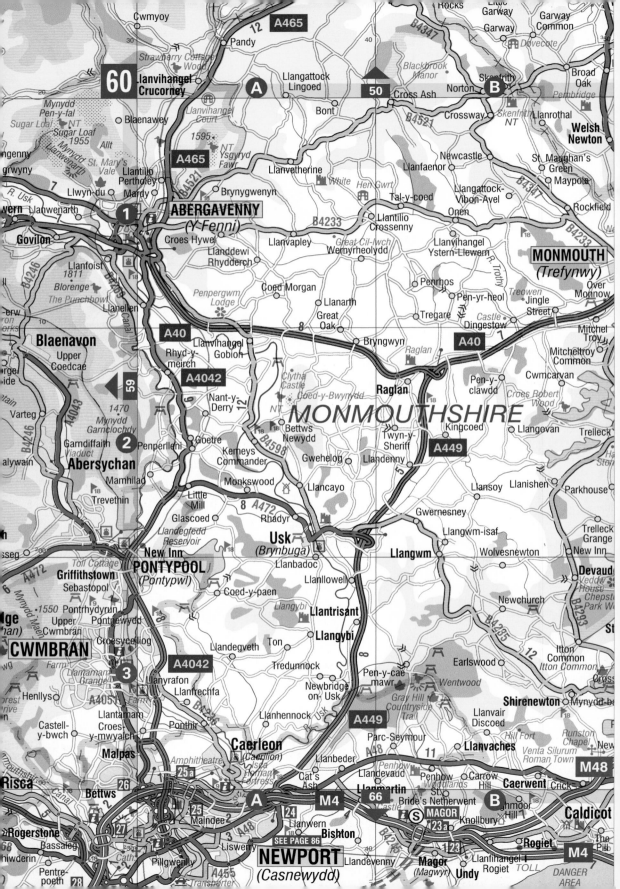

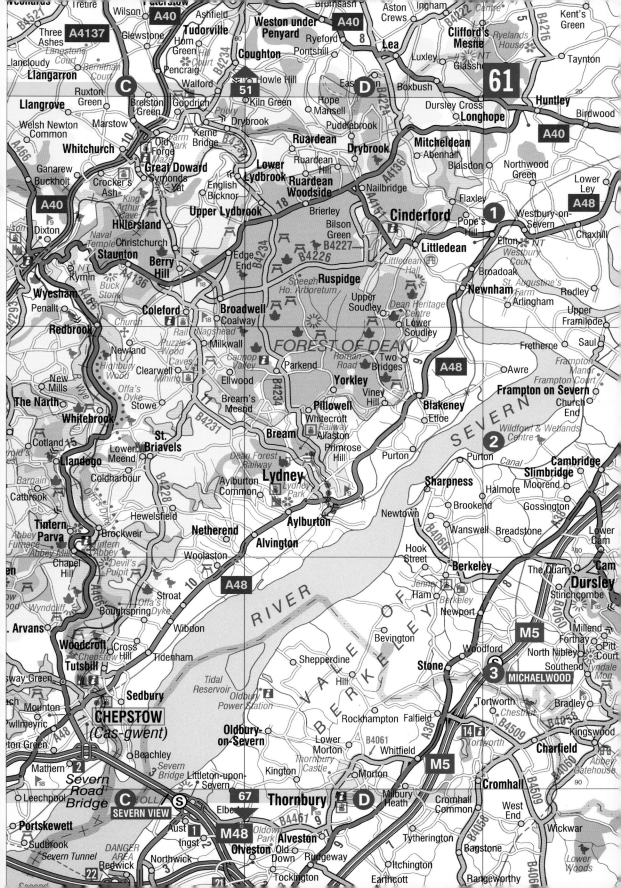

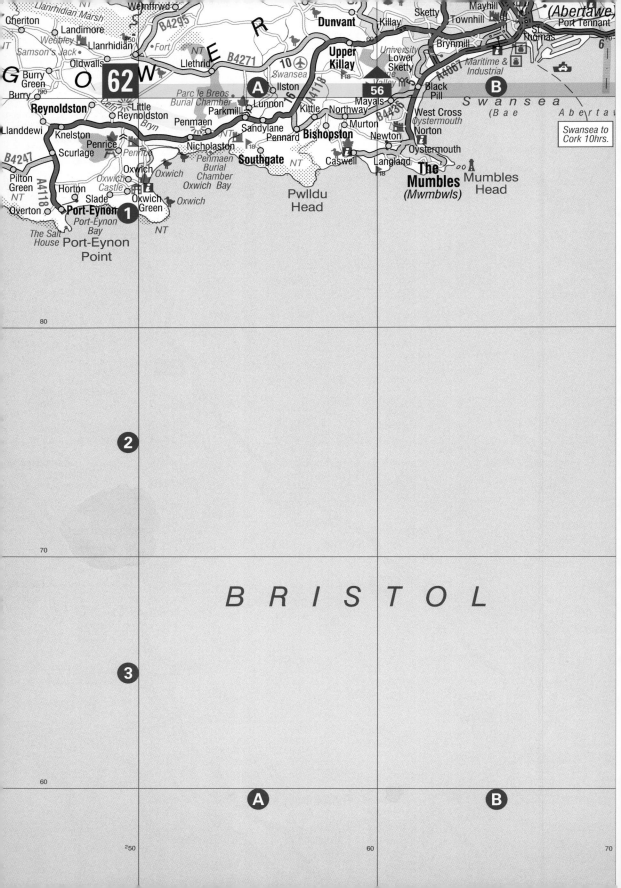

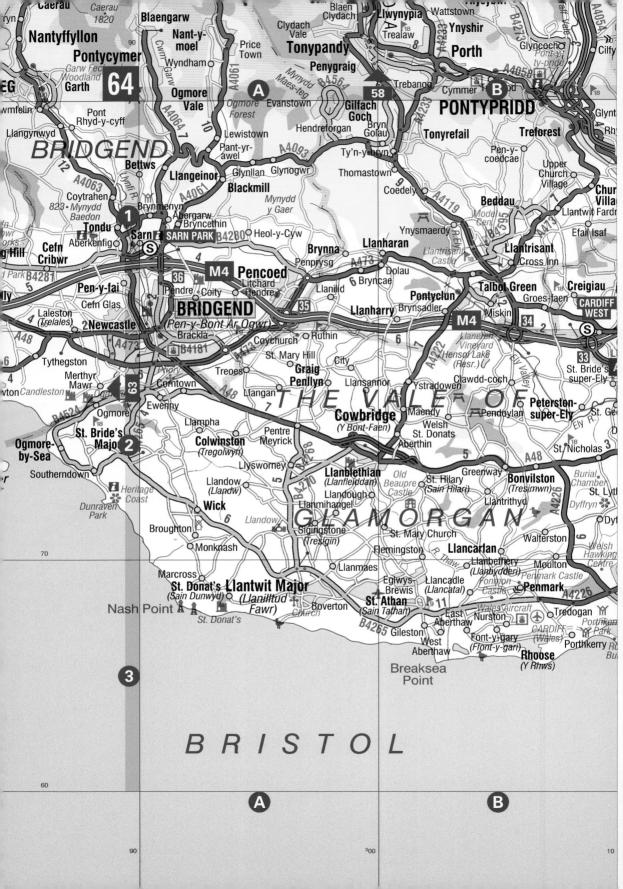

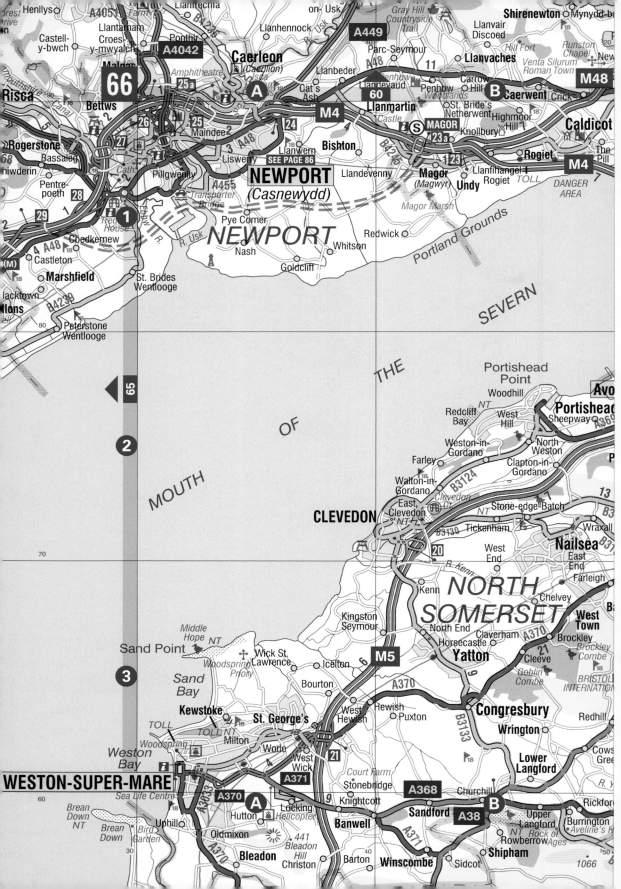

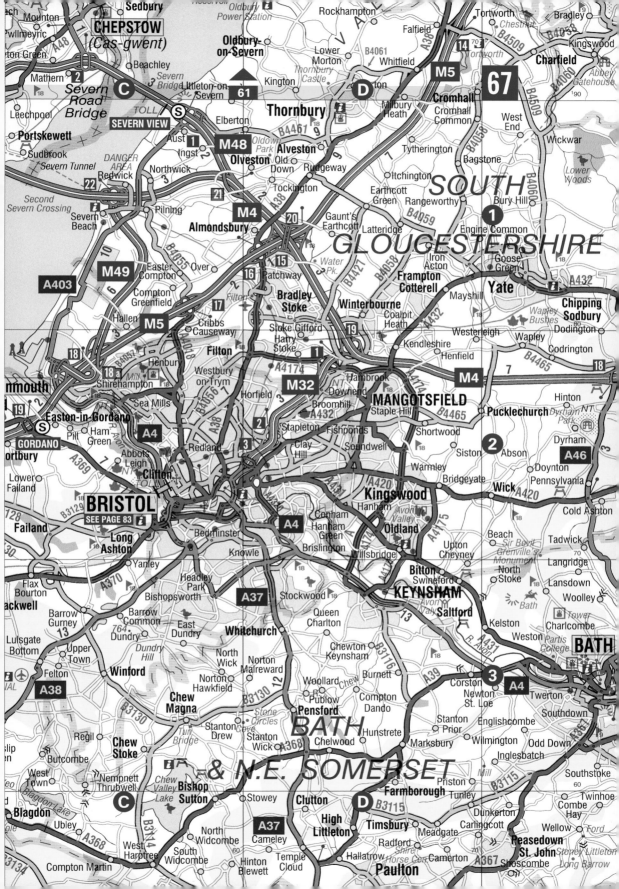

(1) A strict alphabetical order is used e.g Astonlane follows Aston juxta Mondrum but precedes Aston Munslow.

(2) The map reference given refers to the actual map square in which the town spot or built-up area is located and not to the place name.

(3) Where two or more places of the same name occur in the same County or Unitary Authority, the nearest large town is also given;
e.g. Aston. *Ches* . . . . 3C **11** (nr. Frodsham) indicates that Aston is located in square 3C on page **11** and is situated near Frodsham in the County of Cheshire.

Mynegai i Ddinasoedd, Trefi, Pentrefi, Cymydau a Lleoliadau

(1) *Glynir yn gaeth wrth drefn y wyddor e.e. mae Astonlane yn dilyn Aston juxta Mondrum ond yn dod cyn Aston Munslow.*

(2) *Mae'r cyfeirnod map a roddir yn cyfeirio at yr union sgwaryn ar y map lle mae smotyn y dref neu'r ardal adeiliedig ac nid at enw'r lle.*

(3) *Os bydd dau le gyda'r un enw'n digwydd yn yr un Sir neu'r un awdurdod Unedol, rhoddir enw'r dref fawr agosaf hefyd;*
*e.e. Mae Aston. Ches . . . . 3C **11** (nr. Frodsham) yn dangos bod Aston yn sgwaryn 3C ar dudalen **11** a'i bod hi ger Frodsham yn Sydd Gaer.*

COUNTIES AND UNITARY AUTHORITIES with the abbreviations used in this index

Siroedd ac Awdurdodau Unedol gyda'r byrfoddau a ddefnyddir yn y mynegai hwn

Bath & N E Somerset : *Bath*
Blaenau Gwent : *Blae*
Bridgend : *B'end*
Bristol : *Bris*
Caerphilly : *Cphy*
Cardiff : *Card*
Carmarthenshire : *Carm*
Ceredigion : *Cdgn*
Cheshire : *Ches*
Conwy : *Cnwy*
Denbighshire : *Den*
Flintshire : *Flin*
Gloucestershire : *Glos*
Greater Manchester : *G Man*
Gwynedd : *Gwyn*
Halton : *Hal*
Herefordshire : *Here*
Isle of Anglesey : *IOA*
Lancashire : *Lanc*
Merseyside : *Mers*
Merthyr Tydfil : *Mer T*
Monmouthshire : *Mon*
Neath Port Talbot : *Neat*
Newport : *Newp*
North Somerset : *N Som*
Pembrokeshire : *Pemb*
Powys : *Powy*
Rhondda Cynon Taff : *Rhon*
Shropshire : *Shrp*
Somerset : *Som*
South Gloucestershire : *S Glo*
Staffordshire : *Staf*
Swansea : *Swan*
Telford & Wrekin : *Telf*
Torfaen : *Torf*
Vale of Glamorgan, The : *V Glam*
Warrington : *Warr*
Worcestershire : *Worc*
Wrexham : *Wrex*

A

Abberley. *Worc* 2D **41**
Abberley Common. *Worc* 2D **41**
Abbey-cwm-hir. *Powy* 1B **38**
Abbey Dore. *Here* 2A **50**
Abbots Leigh. *N Som* 2C **67**
Abcott. *Shrp* 1A **40**
Abdon. *Shrp* 3C **33**
Abenhall. *Glos* 1D **61**
Aber. *Cdgn* 1D **45**
Aberaeron. *Cdgn* 2D **35**
Aberafan. *Neat* 1C **63**
Aberaman. *Rhon* 2B **58**
Aberangell. *Powy* 3D **23**
Aberarad. *Carm* 2C **45**
Aberarth. *Cdgn* 2D **35**
Aberavon. *Neat* 1C **63**
Aber-banc. *Cdgn* 1C **45**
Aberbargoed. *Cphy* 3C **59**
Aberbechan. *Powy* 2C **31**
Aberbeeg. *Blae* 2D **59**
Aberbowlan. *Carm* 2B **46**
Aberbran. *Powy* 3A **48**
Abercanaid. *Mer T* 2B **58**
Abercarn. *Cphy* 3D **59**
Abercastle. *Pemb* 2B **42**
Abercegir. *Powy* 1D **29**
Abercraf. *Powy* 1D **57**
Abercregan. *Neat* 3D **57**
Abercwmboi. *Rhon* 3B **58**
Abercych. *Pemb* 1B **44**
Abercynon. *Rhon* 3B **58**
Aber-Cywarch. *Gwyn* 3D **23**
Aberdar. *Rhon* 2A **58**
Aberdare. *Rhon* 2A **58**
Aberdaron. *Gwyn* 2A **20**
Aberdaugleddau. *Pemb* 2C **53**
Aberdesach. *Gwyn* 2D **13**
Aberdovey. *Gwyn* 2B **28**
Aberdulais. *Neat* 3C **57**
Aberdyfi. *Gwyn* 2B **28**
Aberedw. *Powy* 1B **48**
Abereiddy. *Pemb* 2A **42**
Abererch. *Gwyn* 1C **21**
Aberfan. *Mer T* 2B **58**
Aberffraw. *IOA* 1C **13**
Aberffrwd. *Cdgn* 1B **36**
Abergarw. *B'end* 1A **64**
Abergarwed. *Neat* 2D **57**
Abergavenny. *Mon* 1A **60**
Abergele. *Cnwy* 3A **8**
Aber-Giar. *Carm* 1A **46**
Abergorlech. *Carm* 2A **46**
Abergwaun. *Pemb* 2C **43**
Abergwesyn. *Powy* 3D **37**
Abergwili. *Carm* 3D **45**
Abergwynfi. *Neat* 3D **57**
Abergwyngregyn. *Gwyn* 3B **6**
Abergynolwyn. *Gwyn* 1B **28**
Aberhafesp. *Powy* 2B **30**
Aberhonddu. *Powy* 3B **48**
Aberhosan. *Powy* 2D **29**
Aberkenfig. *B'end* 1D **63**
Aberllefenni. *Cdgn* 1C **29**
Abermaw. *Gwyn* 3B **22**
Abermeurig. *Cdgn* 3A **36**
Aber-miwl. *Powy* 2C **31**
Abermule. *Powy* 2C **31**
Abernant. *Carm* 3C **45**
Abernant. *Rhon* 2B **58**
Aber-oer. *Wrex* 3D **17**
Aberpennar. *Rhon* 3B **58**
Aberporth. *Cdgn* 3B **34**
Aberriw. *Powy* 1C **31**
Abersoch. *Gwyn* 2C **21**
Abersychan. *Torf* 2D **59**
Abertawe. *Swan* 3B **56**
Aberteifi. *Cdgn* 1A **44**
Aberthin. *V Glam* 2B **64**
Abertillery. *Blae* 2D **59**
Abertridwr. *Cphy* 1C **65**
Abertridwr. *Powy* 3B **24**
Abertyleri. *Blae* 2D **59**
Abertysswg. *Cphy* 2C **59**
Aber Village. *Powy* 3C **49**
Aberyscir. *Powy* 3B **48**
Aberystwyth. *Cdgn* 3A **28**
Abram. *G Man* 1D **11**
Abson. *S Glo* 2D **67**
Aconbury. *Here* 2C **51**
Acrefair. *Wrex* 3D **17**
Acton. *Ches* 2D **19**
Acton. *Shrp* 3A **32**
Acton. *Wrex* 2A **18**
Acton Beauchamp. *Here* 3D **41**
Acton Bridge. *Ches* 3C **11**
Acton Burnell. *Shrp* 1C **33**
Acton Green. *Here* 3D **41**
Acton Pigott. *Shrp* 1C **33**
Acton Round. *Shrp* 2D **33**
Acton Scott. *Shrp* 3B **32**
Adderley. *Shrp* 1D **27**
Adeney. *Telf* 3D **27**
Adfa. *Powy* 1B **30**
Adforton. *Here* 1B **40**
Admaston. *Telf* 3D **27**
Adpar. *Cdgn* 1C **45**
Afon-wen. *Flin* 3C **9**
Aigburth. *Mers* 2A **10**
Ailey. *Here* 1A **50**
Aintree. *Mers* 1A **10**
Alberbury. *Shrp* 3A **26**
Albert Town. *Pemb* 1C **53**
Albrighton. *Shrp* 3B **26**
Alcaston. *Shrp* 3B **32**
Aldersey Green. *Ches* 2B **18**
Alderton. *Shrp* 2B **26**
Aldford. *Ches* 2B **18**
Aldon. *Shrp* 1B **40**
Alfrick. *Worc* 3D **41**
Alfrick Pound. *Worc* 3D **41**
Alkington. *Shrp* 1C **27**
Allaston. *Glos* 2D **61**
Allensmore. *Here* 2B **50**
Allerton. *Mers* 2B **10**
Allscott. *Shrp* 2D **33**
Allscott. *Telf* 3D **27**
All Stretton. *Shrp* 2B **32**
Allt. *Carm* 2A **56**
Alltami. *Flin* 1D **17**
Alltmawr. *Powy* 1B **48**
Alltwalis. *Carm* 2D **45**
Alltwen. *Neat* 2C **57**
Alltyblacca. *Cdgn* 1A **46**
Allt-y-goed. *Pemb* 1A **44**
Almeley. *Here* 3A **40**
Almeley Wooton. *Here* 3A **40**
Almington. *Staf* 1D **27**
Almondsbury. *S Glo* 1D **67**
Alport. *Powy* 2D **31**
Alpraham. *Ches* 2C **19**
Alvanley. *Ches* 3B **10**
Alveston. *S Glo* 1D **67**
Alvington. *Glos* 2D **61**
Ambleston. *Pemb* 3C **43**
Amlwch. *IOA* 1D **5**
Amlwch Port. *IOA* 1D **5**
Ammanford. *Carm* 1B **56**
Amroth. *Pemb* 2A **54**
Anchor. *Shrp* 3C **31**
Anderton. *Ches* 3D **11**
Anelog. *Gwyn* 2A **20**
Anfield. *Mers* 1A **10**
Angelbank. *Shrp* 1C **41**
Angle. *Pemb* 2B **52**
Annscroft. *Shrp* 1B **32**
Antrobus. *Ches* 3D **11**
Appleton. *Hal* 2C **11**
Appleton Thorn. *Warr* 2D **11**
Arberth. *Pemb* 1A **54**
Arddleen. *Powy* 3D **25**
Arddlin. *Powy* 3D **25**
Argoed. *Cphy* 3C **59**
Argoed Mill. *Powy* 2A **38**
Arleston. *Telf* 3D **27**
Arley. *Ches* 2D **11**
Arlingham. *Glos* 1D **61**
Arthog. *Gwyn* 3B **22**
Ashbrook. *Shrp* 2B **32**
Ashfield. *Here* 3C **51**
Ashfield. *Shrp* 3C **33**
Ashford Bowdler. *Shrp* 1C **41**
Ashford Carbonel. *Shrp* 1C **41**
Ashley Heath. *Staf* 1D **27**
Ashley Moor. *Here* 2B **40**
Ash Magna. *Shrp* 1C **27**
Ash Parva. *Shrp* 1C **27**
Ashperton. *Here* 1D **51**
Ashton. *Ches* 1C **19**
Ashton. *Here* 2C **41**
Ashton-in-Makerfield. *G Man* 1C **11**
Asterley. *Shrp* 1A **32**
Asterton. *Shrp* 2A **32**
Astley. *G Man* 1D **11**
Astley. *Shrp* 3C **27**
Astley Abbotts. *Shrp* 2D **33**
Aston. *Ches* 3C **11**
(nr. Frodsham)
Aston. *Ches* 3D **19**
(nr. Nantwich)
Aston. *Flin* 1A **18**
Aston. *Here* 2B **40**
Aston. *Shrp* 2C **27**
Aston. *Staf* 3D **19**
Aston. *Telf* 1D **33**
Aston Botterell. *Shrp* 3D **33**
Aston Crews. *Here* 3D **51**
Aston Eyre. *Shrp* 2D **33**
Aston Ingham. *Here* 3D **51**
Aston juxta Mondrum. *Ches* 2D **19**
Astonlane. *Shrp* 2D **33**
Aston Munslow. *Shrp* 3C **33**
Aston on Clun. *Shrp* 3A **32**
Aston Pigott. *Shrp* 1A **32**
Aston Rogers. *Shrp* 1A **32**
Atcham. *Shrp* 1C **33**
Atherton. *G Man* 1D **11**
Atterley. *Shrp* 2D **33**
Auberrow. *Here* 1B **50**
Audlem. *Ches* 3D **19**
Aulden. *Here* 3B **40**
Aust. *S Glo* 1C **67**
Avonmouth. *Bris* 2C **67**
Awre. *Glos* 2D **61**
Aylburton. *Glos* 2D **61**
Aylburton Common. *Glos* 2D **61**
Aylton. *Here* 2D **51**
Aymestrey. *Here* 2B **40**

B

Babbinswood. *Shrp* 2A **26**
Babel. *Carm* 2D **47**
Babell. *Flin* 3C **9**
Bachau. *IOA* 2D **5**
Bacheldre. *Powy* 2D **31**
Bachymbyd Fawr. *Den* 1B **16**
Backe. *Carm* 1B **54**
Backford. *Ches* 3B **10**
Backwell. *N Som* 3B **66**
Bacton. *Here* 2A **50**
Bae Cinmel. *Cnwy* 2A **8**
Bae Colwyn. *Cnwy* 3D **7**
Bae Penrhyn. *Cnwy* 2D **7**
Bagginswood. *Shrp* 3D **33**
Bagillt. *Flin* 3D **9**
Baglan. *Neat* 3C **57**
Bagley. *Shrp* 2B **26**
Bagstone. *S Glo* 1D **67**
Bagwy Llydiart. *Here* 3B **50**
Bala. *Gwyn* 1A **24**

Balderton. *Ches* 1A **18**
Ball. *Shrp* 2A **26**
Ballingham. *Here* 2C **51**
Bancffosfelen. *Carm* 1D **55**
Bancycapel. *Carm* 1D **55**
Bancyfelin. *Carm* 1C **55**
Banc-y-ffordd. *Carm* 2D **45**
Bangor. *Gwyn* 3A **6**
Bangor-is-y-coed. *Wrex* 3A **18**
Bank Street. *Worc* 2D **41**
Bank, The. *Shrp* 2D **33**
Banwell. *N Som* 3A **66**
Barbridge. *Ches* 2D **19**
Barewood. *Here* 3A **40**
Bargod. *Cphy* 3C **59**
Bargoed. *Cphy* 3C **59**
Barmouth. *Gwyn* 3B **22**
Barnston. *Mers* 2D **9**
Barnton. *Ches* 3D **11**
Barons Cross. *Here* 3B **40**
Barri. *V Glam* 3C **65**
Barrow. *Shrp* 1D **33**
Barrow Common. *N Som* 3C **67**
Barrow Gurney. *N Som* 3C **67**
Barrow Nook. *Lanc* 1B **10**
Barrow's Green. *Ches* 2C **11**
Barry. *V Glam* 3C **65**
Barry Island. *V Glam* 3C **65**
Bartestree. *Here* 1C **51**
Barton. *Ches* 2B **18**
Baschurch. *Shrp* 2B **26**
Bassaleg. *Newp* 1D **65**
Bate Heath. *Ches* 3D **11**
Bath. *Bath* 3D **67**
Battle. *Powy* 2B **48**
Battlefield. *Shrp* 3C **27**
Bayston Hill. *Shrp* 1B **32**
Bayton. *Worc* 1D **41**
Bayton Common. *Worc* 1D **41**
Beach. *S Glo* 2D **67**
Beachley. *Glos* 3C **61**
Bearstone. *Shrp* 1D **27**
Beaufort. *Blae* 1C **59**
Beaumaris. *IOA* 3B **6**
Bebington. *Mers* 2A **10**
Beddau. *Rhon* 1B **64**
Beddgelert. *Gwyn* 3A **14**
Bedford. *G Man* 1D **11**
Bedlinog. *Mer T* 2B **58**
Bedminster. *Bris* 2C **67**
Bedstone. *Shrp* 1A **40**
Bedwas. *Cphy* 1C **65**
Bedwellty. *Cphy* 2C **59**
Beeston. *Ches* 2C **19**
Began. *Card* 1D **65**
Begelly. *Pemb* 2A **54**
Beggar's Bush. *Powy* 2D **39**
Beguildy. *Powy* 1C **39**
Belgrano. *Cnwy* 3A **8**
Belle Vue. *Shrp* 3B **26**
Benllech. *IOA* 2A **6**
Benthall. *Shrp* 1D **33**
Bentlawn. *Shrp* 1A **32**
Berkeley. *Glos* 3D **61**
Berriew. *Powy* 1C **31**
Berrington. *Shrp* 1C **33**
Berrington. *Worc* 2C **41**
Berrington Green. *Worc* 2C **41**
Berrow Green. *Worc* 3D **41**
Berry Hill. *Glos* 1C **61**
Berry Hill. *Pemb* 1D **43**
Bersham. *Wrex* 3A **18**
Berthengam. *Flin* 3C **9**
Berwyn. *Den* 3C **17**
Bethania. *Cdgn* 2A **36**
Bethania. *Gwyn* 3C **15**
   (nr. Blaenau Ffestiniog)
Bethania. *Gwyn* 2B **14**
   (nr. Caernarfon)
Bethel. *Gwyn* 1A **24**
   (nr. Bala)
Bethel. *Gwyn* 1A **14**
   (nr. Caernarfon)
Bethel. *IOA* 3C **5**
Bethesda. *Gwyn* 1B **14**
Bethesda. *Pemb* 1D **53**
Bethlehem. *Carm* 3B **46**
Betley. *Staf* 3D **19**
Bettisfield. *Wrex* 1B **26**
Betton. *Shrp* 1D **27**
Betton Strange. *Shrp* 1C **33**
Bettws. *B'end* 1D **63**
Bettws. *Newp* 3D **59**
Bettws Bledrws. *Cdgn* 3A **36**
Bettws Cedewain. *Powy* 2C **31**
Bettws Gwerfil Goch. *Den* 3B **16**
Bettws Ifan. *Cdgn* 1C **45**
Bettws Newydd. *Mon* 2A **60**
Betws. *Carm* 1B **56**

Betws Garmon. *Gwyn* 2A **14**
Betws-y-Coed. *Cnwy* 2C **15**
Betws-yn-Rhos. *Cnwy* 3A **8**
Beulah. *Cdgn* 1B **44**
Beulah. *Powy* 3A **38**
Bevington. *Glos* 3D **61**
Bickershaw. *G Man* 1D **11**
Bickerton. *Ches* 2C **19**
Bickley Moss. *Ches* 3C **19**
Bicton. *Here* 2B **40**
Bicton. *Shrp* 3D **31**
   (nr. Bishop's Castle)
Bicton. *Shrp* 3B **26**
   (nr. Shrewsbury)
Bicton Heath. *Shrp* 3B **26**
Bidston. *Mers* 2D **9**
Billinge. *Mers* 1C **11**
Billingsley. *Shrp* 3D **33**
Bilson Green. *Glos* 1D **61**
Bings Heath. *Shrp* 3C **27**
Binweston. *Shrp* 1A **32**
Bircher. *Here* 2B **40**
Birchgrove. *Card* 2C **65**
Birchgrove. *Swan* 3C **57**
Birch Heath. *Ches* 1C **19**
Birch Hill. *Ches* 3C **11**
Birchwood. *Warr* 1D **11**
Birdwood. *Glos* 1D **61**
Birkenhead. *Mers* 2A **10**
Birley. *Here* 3B **40**
Birtley. *Here* 2B **40**
Bishop's Castle. *Shrp* 3A **32**
Bishop's Frome. *Here* 1D **51**
Bishopston. *Swan* 1A **62**
Bishopstone. *Here* 1B **50**
Bishop Sutton. *Bath* 2C **67**
Bishopsworth. *Bris* 3C **67**
Bishton. *Newp* 1A **66**
Bitterley. *Shrp* 1C **41**
Bitton. *S Glo* 3D **67**
Blackbrook. *Mers* 1C **11**
Blackford. *Shrp* 3C **33**
Blackmill. *B'end* 1A **64**
Blackmoor. *G Man* 1D **11**
Black Pill. *Swan* 3B **56**
Blackrock. *Mon* 1C **59**
Black Tar. *Pemb* 2C **53**
Blacktown. *Newp* 1D **65**
Blackwood. *Cphy* 3C **59**
Blacon. *Ches* 1A **18**
Blaenannerch. *Cdgn* 1B **44**
Blaenau Dolwyddelan. *Cnwy* 2B **14**
Blaenau Ffestiniog. *Gwyn* 3C **15**
Blaenavon. *Torf* 2D **59**
Blaenawey. *Mon* 1D **59**
Blaen Celyn. *Cdgn* 3C **35**
Blaen Clydach. *Rhon* 3A **58**
Blaendulais. *Neat* 2D **57**
Blaenffos. *Pemb* 2A **44**
Blaengarw. *B'end* 3A **58**
Blaen-geuffordd. *Cdgn* 3B **28**
Blaengwrach. *Neat* 2D **57**
Blaengwynfi. *Neat* 3A **58**
Blaenllechau. *Rhon* 3B **58**
Blaenpennal. *Cdgn* 2B **36**
Blaenplwyf. *Cdgn* 1A **36**
Blaenporth. *Cdgn* 1B **44**
Blaenrhondda. *Rhon* 3A **58**
Blaenwaun. *Carm* 3B **44**
Blaen-y-coed. *Carm* 2C **45**
Blaenycwm. *Rhon* 3A **58**
Blagdon. *N Som* 3C **67**
Blaina. *Blae* 2D **59**
Blaisdon. *Glos* 1D **61**
Blakemere. *Here* 1A **50**
Blakeney. *Glos* 2D **61**
Blakenhall. *Ches* 3D **19**
Bleadon. *N Som* 3A **66**
Bleddfa. *Powy* 2D **39**
Bletchley. *Shrp* 1D **27**
Bletherston. *Pemb* 3D **43**
Bliss Gate. *Worc* 1D **41**
Blists Hill. *Telf* 1D **33**
Blue Anchor. *Swan* 3A **56**
Bodedern. *IOA* 2C **5**
Bodelwyddan. *Den* 3B **8**
Bodenham. *Here* 3C **41**
Bodewryd. *IOA* 1C **5**
Bodfari. *Den* 3B **8**
Bodffordd. *IOA* 3D **5**
Bodnant. *Cnwy* 3D **7**
Bodorgan. *IOA* 1A **10**
Boduan. *Gwyn* 1C **21**
Bog, The. *Shrp* 2A **32**
Bold Heath. *Mers* 2C **11**
Bolstone. *Here* 2C **51**
Bomere Heath. *Shrp* 3C **27**
Boncath. *Pemb* 2B **44**
Bont. *Mon* 1A **60**

Bontddu. *Gwyn* 3B **22**
Bont Dolgadfan. *Powy* 1D **29**
Bontgoch. *Cdgn* 3B **28**
Bontnewydd. *Cdgn* 2B **36**
Bont-newydd. *Cnwy* 3B **8**
Bontnewydd. *Gwyn* 1D **13**
   (nr. Caernarfon)
Bont Newydd. *Gwyn* 3C **15**
   (nr. Ffestiniog)
Bontuchel. *Den* 2B **16**
Bonvilston. *V Glam* 2B **64**
Bon-y-maen. *Swan* 3B **56**
Booley. *Shrp* 2C **27**
Boothstown. *G Man* 1D **11**
Bootle. *Mers* 1A **10**
Boraston. *Shrp* 1D **41**
Boreton. *Shrp* 1C **33**
Borras Head. *Wrex* 2A **18**
Borth. *Cdgn* 3B **28**
Borth-y-Gest. *Gwyn* 1A **22**
Bosbury. *Here* 1D **51**
Bosherston. *Pemb* 3C **53**
Bostock Green. *Ches* 1D **19**
Botloe's Green. *Glos* 3D **51**
Botwnnog. *Gwyn* 1C **21**
Boughrood. *Powy* 2C **49**
Boughspring. *Glos* 3C **61**
Bouldon. *Shrp* 3C **33**
Boulston. *Pemb* 1C **53**
Bounds. *Here* 2D **51**
Bourton. *N Som* 3A **66**
Bourton. *Shrp* 2C **33**
Boverton. *V Glam* 3A **64**
Bowley. *Here* 3C **41**
Bowling Bank. *Wrex* 3B **18**
Bow Street. *Cdgn* 3B **28**
Boxbush. *Glos* 3D **51**
Brackla. *B'end* 2A **64**
Bradfield Green. *Ches* 2D **19**
Bradley. *Ches* 3C **11**
Bradley. *Glos* 3D **61**
Bradley. *Wrex* 2A **18**
Bradley Green. *Ches* 3C **19**
Bradley Stoke. *S Glo* 1D **67**
Bradlow. *Here* 2D **51**
Braichmelyn. *Gwyn* 1B **14**
Brampton Abbotts. *Here* 3D **51**
Brampton Bryan. *Here* 1A **40**
Brand Green. *Glos* 3D **51**
Brandhill. *Shrp* 1B **40**
Bransley. *Shrp* 1C **41**
Bratton. *Telf* 3D **27**
Breaden Heath. *Shrp* 1B **26**
Breadstone. *Glos* 2D **61**
Bream. *Glos* 2D **61**
Bream's Meend. *Glos* 2D **61**
Brechfa. *Carm* 2A **46**
Brecon. *Powy* 3B **48**
Bredenbury. *Here* 3D **41**
Bredwardine. *Here* 1A **50**
Breinton. *Here* 2B **50**
Breinton Common. *Here* 2B **50**
Brelston Green. *Here* 3C **51**
Bretton. *Flin* 1A **18**
Bridell. *Pemb* 1A **44**
Bridgemere. *Ches* 3D **19**
Bridgend. *B'end* 1A **64**
Bridge Sollers. *Here* 1B **50**
Bridge Trafford. *Ches* 3B **10**
Bridgeyate. *S Glo* 2D **67**
Bridgnorth. *Shrp* 2D **33**
Bridstow. *Here* 3C **51**
Brierley. *Glos* 1D **61**
Brierley. *Here* 3B **40**
Brilley. *Here* 1D **49**
Brimaston. *Pemb* 3C **43**
Brimfield. *Here* 2C **41**
Brimstage. *Mers* 2A **10**
Brinsty Common. *Here* 3D **41**
Brislington. *S Glo* 2C **67**
Bristol. *Bris* 2C **67**
Bristol International Airport.
   N Som 3C **67**
Brithdir. *Cphy* 2C **59**
Brithdir. *Cdgn* 1C **45**
Brithdir. *Gwyn* 3C **23**
Briton Ferry. *Neat* 3C **57**
Broadfield. *Pemb* 2A **54**
Broad Haven. *Pemb* 1B **52**
Broadheath. *Worc* 2D **41**
Broadlay. *Carm* 2D **53**
Broadmoor. *Pemb* 2A **54**
Broad Oak. *Carm* 3A **46**
Broadoak. *Glos* 1D **61**
Broad Oak. *Here* 3B **50**
Broadstone. *Shrp* 3C **33**
Broad, The. *Here* 2B **40**
Broadway. *Carm* 2C **55**
   (nr. Kidwelly)

Broadway. *Carm* 1B **54**
   (nr. Laugharne)
Broadway. *Pemb* 1B **52**
Broadwell. *Glos* 1C **61**
Brobury. *Here* 1A **50**
Brockhampton. *Here* 2C **51**
Brockley. *N Som* 3B **66**
Brockton. *Shrp* 3A **32**
   (nr. Bishop's Castle)
Brockton. *Shrp* 1D **33**
   (nr. Madeley)
Brockton. *Shrp* 2C **33**
   (nr. Much Wenlock)
Brockton. *Shrp* 1A **32**
   (nr. Pontesbury)
Brockton. *Telf* 3D **27**
Brockweir. *Glos* 2C **61**
Bromborough. *Mers* 2A **10**
Bromdon. *Shrp* 3D **33**
Bromfield. *Shrp* 1B **40**
Bromley. *Shrp* 2D **33**
Brompton. *Shrp* 1C **33**
Bromsash. *Here* 3D **51**
Bromsberrow Heath. *Glos* 2D **51**
Bromyard. *Here* 3D **41**
Bromyard Downs. *Here* 3D **41**
Bronaber. *Gwyn* 1C **23**
Broncroft. *Shrp* 3C **33**
Brongest. *Cdgn* 1C **45**
Brongwyn. *Cdgn* 1B **44**
Bronington. *Wrex* 1B **26**
Bronllys. *Powy* 2C **49**
Bronnant. *Cdgn* 2B **36**
Bronwydd Arms. *Carm* 3D **45**
Bronydd. *Powy* 1D **49**
Bronygarth. *Shrp* 1D **25**
Brook. *Carm* 2B **54**
Brookend. *Glos* 2D **61**
Brookhurst. *Mers* 2A **10**
Brooklands. *Shrp* 3C **19**
Brooks. *Powy* 2C **31**
Broome. *Shrp* 2C **33**
   (nr. Cardington)
Broome. *Shrp* 3B **32**
   (nr. Craven Arms)
Broomedge. *Warr* 2D **11**
Broomhill. *Bris* 2D **67**
Broom's Green. *Glos* 2D **51**
Broseley. *Shrp* 1D **33**
Broughall. *Shrp* 3C **19**
Broughton. *Flin* 1A **18**
Broughton. *V Glam* 2A **64**
Brownhill. *Shrp* 2B **26**
Brownhills. *Shrp* 1D **27**
Brown Knowl. *Ches* 2B **18**
Broxton. *Ches* 2B **18**
Broxwood. *Here* 3A **40**
Bruera. *Ches* 1B **18**
Brymbo. *Cnwy* 3D **7**
Brymbo. *Wrex* 2D **17**
Bryn. *Carm* 2A **56**
Bryn. *G Man* 1C **11**
Bryn. *Neat* 3D **57**
Bryn. *Shrp* 3D **31**
Brynamman. *Carm* 1C **57**
Brynberian. *Pemb* 2A **44**
Brynbryddan. *Neat* 3C **57**
Bryncae. *Rhon* 1A **64**
Bryncethin. *B'end* 1A **64**
Bryncir. *Gwyn* 3D **13**
Bryn-coch. *Neat* 3C **57**
Bryncroes. *Gwyn* 1B **20**
Bryncrug. *Gwyn* 1B **28**
Bryn Du. *IOA* 3C **5**
Bryn Eden. *Gwyn* 2C **23**
Bryneglwys. *Den* 3C **17**
Bryn Eglwys. *Gwyn* 1B **14**
Brynford. *Flin* 3C **9**
Bryn Gates. *G Man* 1C **11**
Bryn Golau. *Rhon* 1B **64**
Bryngwran. *IOA* 3C **5**
Bryngwyn. *Mon* 2A **60**
Bryngwyn. *Powy* 1C **49**
Bryn-henllan. *Pemb* 2D **43**
Brynhoffnant. *Cdgn* 3C **35**
Bryn-llwyn. *Flin* 2B **8**
Brynllywarch. *Powy* 3C **31**
Bryn-mawr. *Blae* 1C **59**
Bryn-mawr. *Gwyn* 1B **20**
Brynmenyn. *B'end* 1A **64**
Brynmill. *Swan* 3B **56**
Brynna. *Rhon* 1A **64**
Brynrefail. *Gwyn* 1A **14**
Brynrefail. *IOA* 2D **5**
Brynsadler. *Rhon* 1B **64**
Bryn-Saith Marchog. *Den* 2B **16**
Brynsiencyn. *IOA* 1D **13**
Brynteg. *IOA* 2D **5**
Brynteg. *Wrex* 2A **18**

Brynygwenyn. *Mon* 1A 60
Bryn-y-maen. *Cnwy* 3D 7
Buckholt. *Here* 1C 61
Buckland. *Here* 3C 41
Buckley. *Flin* 1D 17
Buckley Hill. *Mers* 1A 10
Bucklow Hill. *Ches* 2D 11
Bucknell. *Shrp* 1A 40
Buckton. *Here* 1A 40
Buerton. *Ches* 3D 19
Buildwas. *Shrp* 1D 33
Builth Road. *Powy* 3B 38
Builth Wells. *Powy* 3B 38
Bulkeley. *Ches* 2C 19
Bull Bay. *IOA* 1D 5
Bullinghope. *Here* 2C 51
Bunbury. *Ches* 2C 19
Burcher. *Here* 2A 40
Burcote. *Shrp* 2D 33
Burford. *Shrp* 2C 41
Burghill. *Here* 1B 50
Burland. *Ches* 2D 19
Burley Gate. *Here* 1C 51
Burlingjobb. *Powy* 3D 39
Burlton. *Shrp* 2B 26
Burnett. *Bath* 3D 67
Burnleydam. *Wrex* 3D 19
Burrington. *Here* 1B 40
Burrington. *N Som* 3B 66
Burry. *Swan* 3D 55
Burry Green. *Swan* 3D 55
Burry Port. *Carm* 2D 55
Burton. *Ches* 1C 19
   (nr. Kelsall)
Burton. *Ches* 3A 10
   (nr. Neston)
Burton. *Pemb* 2C 53
Burton. *Wrex* 2A 18
Burton Green. *Wrex* 2A 18
Burtonwood. *Warr* 1C 11
Burwardsley. *Ches* 2C 19
Burwarton. *Shrp* 3D 33
Burwen. *IOA* 1D 5
Bury Hill. *S Glo* 1D 67
Bush Bank. *Here* 3B 40
Bushmoor. *Shrp* 3B 32
Butcombe. *N Som* 3C 67
Bute Town. *Cphy* 2C 59
Butt Green. *Ches* 2D 19
Buttington. *Powy* 1D 31
Buttonbridge. *Shrp* 1D 41
Buttonoak. *Shrp* 1D 41
Bwcle. *Flin* 1D 17
Bwlch. *Powy* 3C 49
Bwlchderwin. *Gwyn* 3D 13
Bwlchgwyn. *Wrex* 2D 17
Bwlch-Llan. *Cdgn* 3A 36
Bwlchnewydd. *Carm* 3C 45
Bwlchtocyn. *Gwyn* 2C 21
Bwlch-y-cibau. *Powy* 3C 25
Bwlchyddar. *Powy* 2C 25
Bwlch-y-fadfa. *Cdgn* 1D 45
Bwlch-y-ffridd. *Powy* 2B 30
Bwlch y Garreg. *Powy* 2B 30
Bwlch-y-groes. *Pemb* 2B 44
Bwlch-yr-haiarn. *Cnwy* 2C 15
Bwlch-y-sarnau. *Powy* 1B 38
Byford. *Here* 1A 50
Bylchau. *Cnwy* 1A 16
Byley. *Ches* 1D 19
Bynea. *Carm* 3A 56
Byton. *Here* 2A 40

C

Cadishead. *G Man* 1D 11
Cadole. *Flin* 1D 17
Cadoxton-Juxta-Neath. *Neat* 3C 57
Cadwst. *Den* 1B 24
Caeathro. *Gwyn* 1A 14
Caehopkin. *Powy* 1D 57
Caerau. *B'end* 3D 57
Caerau. *Card* 2C 65
Cae'r-bont. *Powy* 1D 57
Cae'r-bryn. *Carm* 1A 56
Caerdeon. *Gwyn* 3B 22
Caerdydd. *Card* 2C 65
Caerfarchell. *Pemb* 3A 42
Caerffili. *Cphy* 1C 65
Caerfyrddin. *Carm* 1D 55
Caergeiliog. *IOA* 3C 5
Caergwrle. *Flin* 2A 18
Caergybi. *IOA* 2B 4
Caerleon. *Newp* 3A 60
Caerllion. *Newp* 3B 44
Caerllion. *Newp* 3A 60
Caernarfon. *Gwyn* 1D 13
Caerphilly. *Cphy* 1C 65

Caersws. *Powy* 2B 30
Caerwedros. *Cdgn* 3C 35
Caerwent. *Mon* 3B 60
Caerwys. *Flin* 3C 9
Caim. *IOA* 2B 6
Caio. *Carm* 2B 46
Calcott. *Shrp* 3B 26
Caldicot. *Mon* 1B 66
Caldy. *Mers* 2D 9
Caledfwlch. *Carm* 3B 46
Callaughton. *Shrp* 2D 33
Callow. *Here* 2B 50
Callow Hill. *Worc* 1D 41
Calveley. *Ches* 2C 19
Calverhall. *Shrp* 1D 27
Cam. *Glos* 3D 61
Cambridge. *Glos* 2D 61
Cameley. *Bath* 3D 67
Camerton. *Bath* 3D 67
Camrose. *Pemb* 1C 53
Canaston Bridge. *Pemb* 1D 53
Canon Bridge. *Here* 1B 50
Canon Frome. *Here* 1D 51
Canon Pyon. *Here* 1B 50
Cantlop. *Shrp* 1C 33
Canton. *Card* 2C 65
Capel Bangor. *Cdgn* 3B 28
Capel Betws Lleucu. *Cdgn* 3B 36
Capel Coch. *IOA* 2D 5
Capel Curig. *Cnwy* 2C 15
Capel Cynon. *Cdgn* 1C 45
Capel Dewi. *Carm* 3D 45
Capel Dewi. *Cdgn* 3B 28
   (nr. Aberystwyth)
Capel Dewi. *Cdgn* 1D 45
   (nr. Llandysul)
Capel Garmon. *Cnwy* 2D 15
Capel Gwyn. *IOA* 3C 5
Capel Gwynfe. *Carm* 3C 47
Capel Hendre. *Carm* 1A 56
Capel Isaac. *Carm* 3A 46
Capel Iwan. *Carm* 2B 44
Capel Llanilterne. *Card* 2B 64
Capel Mawr. *IOA* 3D 5
Capel Newydd. *Pemb* 2B 44
Capel Seion. *Carm* 1A 56
Capel Seion. *Cdgn* 1B 36
Capel Uchaf. *Gwyn* 3D 13
Capel-y-ffin. *Powy* 2D 49
Capenhurst. *Ches* 3A 10
Cardeston. *Shrp* 3A 26
Cardiff. *Card* 2C 65
Cardiff Airport. *V Glam* 3B 64
Cardigan. *Cdgn* 1A 44
Cardington. *Shrp* 2C 33
Carew. *Pemb* 2D 53
Carew Cheriton. *Pemb* 2D 53
Carew Newton. *Pemb* 2D 53
Carey. *Here* 2C 51
Carlingcott. *Bath* 3D 67
Carmarthen. *Carm* 1D 55
Carmel. *Carm* 1A 56
Carmel. *Flin* 3C 9
Carmel. *Gwyn* 2D 13
Carmel. *IOA* 2C 5
Carnhedryn. *Pemb* 3A 42
Carno. *Powy* 2A 30
Carreglefn. *IOA* 2C 5
Carrington. *G Man* 1D 11
Carrog. *Cnwy* 3C 15
Carrog. *Den* 3C 17
Carrow Hill. *Mon* 3B 60
Carway. *Carm* 2D 55
Cascob. *Powy* 2D 39
Cas-Mael. *Pemb* 3D 43
Casnewydd. *Newp* 1A 66
Castell. *Cnwy* 1C 15
Castell. *Den* 1C 17
Castell Hendre. *Pemb* 3D 43
Castell-nedd. *Neat* 3C 57
Castell Newydd Emlyn.
   Carm 1C 45
Castell-y-bwch. *Torf* 3D 59
Castlebythe. *Pemb* 3D 43
Castle Caereinion. *Powy* 1C 31
Castle Frome. *Here* 1D 51
Castlemartin. *Pemb* 3C 53
Castlemorris. *Pemb* 2C 43
Castleton. *Newp* 1D 65
Caswell. *Swan* 1A 62
Catbrook. *Mon* 2A 60
Cathedine. *Powy* 3C 49
Catherton. *Shrp* 1D 41
Cat's Ash. *Newp* 3A 60
Caynham. *Shrp* 1C 41
Cefn Berain. *Cnwy* 1A 16
Cefn-brith. *Cnwy* 2A 16
Cefn-bryn-brain. *Carm* 1C 57

Cefn Bychan. *Cphy* 3D 59
Cefn-bychan. *Flin* 1C 17
Cefncaeau. *Carm* 3A 56
Cefn Canol. *Powy* 1D 25
Cefn-coch. *Powy* 2C 25
Cefn-coed-y-cymmer. *Mer T* 2B 58
Cefn Cribwr. *B'end* 1D 63
Cefn-ddwysarn. *Gwyn* 1A 24
Cefn Einion. *Shrp* 3D 31
Cefneithin. *Carm* 1A 56
Cefn Glas. *B'end* 1D 63
Cefngorwydd. *Powy* 1A 48
Cefn Llwyd. *Cdgn* 3B 28
Cefn-mawr. *Wrex* 3D 17
Cefn-y-bedd. *Wrex* 2A 18
Cefn-y-coed. *Powy* 1C 31
Cefn-y-pant. *Carm* 3A 44
Cegidfa. *Powy* 3D 25
Ceinewydd. *Cdgn* 3C 35
Cellan. *Cdgn* 1B 46
Cemaes. *IOA* 1C 5
Cemmaes. *Powy* 1D 29
Cemmaes Road. *Powy* 1D 29
Cenarth. *Carm* 1B 44
Cenin. *Gwyn* 3D 13
Ceri. *Powy* 3C 31
Cerist. *Powy* 3A 30
Cerrigceinwen. *IOA* 3D 5
Cerrigydrudion. *Cnwy* 3A 16
Ceunant. *Gwyn* 1A 14
Chadwick Green. *Mers* 1C 11
Chancery. *Cdgn* 1A 36
Chapel Hill. *Mon* 2C 61
Chapel Lawn. *Shrp* 3D 31
Charfield. *S Glo* 3D 61
Charlcombe. *Bath* 3D 67
Charlton. *Telf* 3C 27
Chatwall. *Shrp* 2C 33
Chaxhill. *Glos* 1D 61
Checkley. *Ches* 3D 19
Checkley. *Here* 2C 51
Chelmarsh. *Shrp* 3D 33
Chelmick. *Shrp* 2B 32
Chelvey. *N Som* 3B 66
Chelwood. *Bath* 3D 67
Cheney Longville. *Shrp* 3B 32
Chepstow. *Mon* 3C 61
Cheriton. *Pemb* 3C 53
Cheriton. *Swan* 3D 55
Cherrington. *Telf* 2D 27
Chester. *Ches* 1B 18
Cheswardine. *Shrp* 2D 27
Cheswell. *Telf* 3D 27
Chetton. *Shrp* 2D 33
Chetwynd Aston. *Telf* 3D 27
Chew Magna. *Bath* 3C 67
Chew Stoke. *Bath* 3C 67
Chewton Keynsham. *Bath* 3D 67
Chickward. *Here* 3D 39
Childer Thornton. *Ches* 3A 10
Child's Ercall. *Shrp* 2D 27
Childwall. *Mers* 2B 10
Chipnall. *Shrp* 1D 27
Chipping Sodbury. *S Glo* 1D 67
Chirbury. *Shrp* 2D 31
Chirk. *Wrex* 1D 25
Cholstrey. *Here* 3B 40
Chorley. *Ches* 2C 19
Chorley. *Shrp* 3D 33
Chorlton. *Ches* 2D 19
Chorlton Lane. *Ches* 3B 18
Choulton. *Shrp* 3A 32
Christchurch. *Glos* 1C 61
Christleton. *Ches* 1B 18
Christon. *N Som* 3A 66
Church Aston. *Telf* 3D 27
Church End. *Glos* 2D 61
Church Hill. *Ches* 1D 19
Churchill. *N Som* 3B 66
Church Minshull. *Ches* 1D 19
Church Preen. *Shrp* 2C 33
Church Pulverbatch. *Shrp* 1B 32
Church Stoke. *Powy* 2D 31
Church Stretton. *Shrp* 2B 32
Churchtown. *Powy* 3D 31
Church Village. *Rhon* 1B 64
Churton. *Ches* 2B 18
Chwilog. *Gwyn* 1D 21
Chwitffordd. *Flin* 3C 9
Cilan Uchaf. *Gwyn* 2B 20
Cilcain. *Flin* 1C 17
Cilcennin. *Cdgn* 3A 36
Cilfrew. *Neat* 2C 57
Cilfynydd. *Rhon* 3B 58
Cilgerran. *Pemb* 1A 44
Cilgeti. *Pemb* 2A 54
Cilgwyn. *Carm* 3C 47
Cilgwyn. *Pemb* 2D 43
Ciliau Aeron. *Cdgn* 3D 35

Cilmaengwyn. *Neat* 2C 57
Cilmeri. *Powy* 3B 38
Cilmery. *Powy* 3B 38
Cilrhedyn. *Pemb* 2B 44
Cilsan. *Carm* 3A 46
Ciltalgarth. *Gwyn* 3D 15
Ciltwrch. *Powy* 1C 49
Cilybebyll. *Neat* 2C 57
Cilycwm. *Carm* 2C 47
Cimla. *Neat* 3C 57
Cinderford. *Glos* 1D 61
Cippyn. *Pemb* 1A 44
City. *Powy* 2D 31
City. *V Glam* 2A 64
City Dulas. *IOA* 2D 5
Clapton-in-Gordano.
   N Som 2B 66
Clarbeston. *Pemb* 3D 43
Clarbeston Road. *Pemb* 3D 43
Clatter. *Powy* 2A 30
Claughton. *Mers* 2A 10
Claverham. *N Som* 3B 66
Clawdd-coch. *V Glam* 2B 64
Clawdd-newydd. *Den* 2B 16
Clay Hill. *Bris* 2D 67
Clearwell. *Glos* 2C 61
Cleedownton. *Shrp* 3C 33
Cleehill. *Shrp* 1C 41
Cleestanton. *Shrp* 1C 41
Clee St Margaret. *Shrp* 3C 33
Cleeton St Mary. *Shrp* 1D 41
Cleeve. *N Som* 3B 66
Clehonger. *Here* 2B 50
Cleobury Mortimer. *Shrp* 1D 41
Cleobury North. *Shrp* 3D 33
Clevedon. *N Som* 2B 66
Clifford. *Here* 1D 49
Clifford's Mesne. *Glos* 3D 51
Clifton. *Bris* 2C 67
Clifton Hill. *Worc* 2D 41
Clifton-upon-Teme. *Worc* 2D 41
Clipiau. *Gwyn* 3D 23
Clive. *Shrp* 2C 27
Clocaenog. *Den* 2B 16
Clock Face. *Mers* 1C 11
Cloddiau. *Powy* 1D 31
Clodock. *Here* 3A 50
Clotton. *Ches* 1C 19
Clows Top. *Worc* 1D 41
Cloy. *Wrex* 3A 18
Cluddley. *Telf* 1D 33
Clun. *Shrp* 3A 32
Clunbury. *Shrp* 3A 32
Clunderwen. *Carm* 1A 54
Clungunford. *Shrp* 1A 40
Clunton. *Shrp* 3A 32
Clutton. *Bath* 3D 67
Clutton. *Ches* 2B 18
Clwt-y-bont. *Gwyn* 1A 14
Clwydfagwyr. *Mer T* 2B 58
Clydach. *Mon* 1D 59
Clydach. *Swan* 2B 56
Clydach Vale. *Rhon* 3A 58
Clydey. *Pemb* 2B 44
Clyne. *Neat* 2D 57
Clynnog-fawr. *Gwyn* 3D 13
Clyro. *Powy* 1D 49
Cnwcau. *Pemb* 1B 44
Cnwch Coch. *Cdgn* 1B 36
Coalbrookdale. *Telf* 1D 33
Coalbrookvale. *Blae* 2D 59
Coalpit Heath. *S Glo* 1D 67
Coalport. *Telf* 1D 33
Coalway. *Glos* 1C 61
Cobhall Common. *Here* 2B 50
Cobnash. *Here* 3B 40
Cock Bank. *Wrex* 3A 18
Cock Gate. *Here* 2B 40
Cockshutford. *Shrp* 3C 33
Cockshutt. *Shrp* 2B 26
Cockyard. *Here* 2B 50
Coddington. *Ches* 2B 18
Coddington. *Here* 1D 51
Codrington. *S Glo* 1D 67
Coed Duon. *Cphy* 3C 59
Coedely. *Rhon* 1B 64
Coedglasson. *Powy* 2B 38
Coedkernew. *Newp* 1D 65
Coed Morgan. *Mon* 1A 60
Coedpoeth. *Wrex* 2D 17
Coedway. *Powy* 3A 26
Coed-y-bryn. *Cdgn* 1C 45
Coed-y-paen. *Mon* 3A 60
Coed-yr-ynys. *Powy* 3C 49
Coed Ystumgwern. *Gwyn* 2A 22
Coelbren. *Powy* 1D 57
Cogan. *V Glam* 2C 65
Coity. *B'end* 1A 64
Cold Ashton. *S Glo* 2D 67

Cold Blow. Pemb ...1A 54
Coldharbour. Glos ...2C 61
Cold Hatton. Telf ...2D 27
Cold Hatton Heath. Telf ...2D 27
Coldwell. Here ...2B 50
Colebatch. Shrp ...3A 32
Coleford. Glos ...1C 61
Colemere. Shrp ...1B 26
Colemore Green. Shrp ...2D 33
Collins Green. Warr ...1C 11
Collins Green. Worc ...3D 41
Colwall Green. Here ...1D 51
Colwall Stone. Here ...1D 51
Colwinston. V Glam ...2A 64
Colwyn Bay. Cnwy ...3D 7
Combe. Here ...2A 40
Combe Hay. Bath ...3D 67
Combe Moor. Here ...2A 40
Comberbach. Ches ...3D 11
Comberton. Here ...2B 40
Comins Coch. Cdgn ...3B 28
Comley. Shrp ...2B 32
Commins. Powy ...2C 25
Commins Coch. Powy ...1D 29
Common Hill. Here ...2C 51
Commonside. Ches ...3C 11
Compton Dando. Bath ...3D 67
Compton Greenfield. S Glo ...1C 67
Compton Martin. Bath ...3C 67
Condover. Shrp ...1B 32
Congl-y-wal. Gwyn ...3C 15
Congresbury. N Som ...3B 66
Conham. S Glo ...2D 67
Connah's Quay. Flin ...1D 17
Conwy. Cnwy ...3C 7
Coppenhall. Ches ...2D 19
Coppenhall Moss. Ches ...2D 19
Coppicegate. Shrp ...3D 33
Coptiviney. Shrp ...1B 26
Coreley. Shrp ...1D 41
Corfton. Shrp ...3B 32
Corlannau. Neat ...3C 57
Corntown. V Glam ...2A 64
Corris. Powy ...1C 29
Corris Uchaf. Gwyn ...1C 29
Corston. Bath ...3D 67
Corwen. Den ...3B 16
Cosheston. Pemb ...2D 53
Cosmeston. V Glam ...3C 65
Cotebrook. Ches ...1C 19
Cotland. Mon ...2C 61
Coton Hill. Shrp ...3B 26
Cotonwood. Here ...1C 27
Coughton. Here ...3C 51
Cound. Shrp ...1C 33
Court Henry. Carm ...3A 46
Cowbridge. V Glam ...2A 64
Cowslip Green. N Som ...3B 66
Coxall. Here ...1A 40
Coxbank. Ches ...3D 19
Coychurch. V Glam ...1A 64
Coytrahen. B'end ...1D 63
Crabtree Green. Wrex ...3A 18
Crackleybank. Shrp ...3D 27
Cradley. Here ...1D 51
Cradoc. Powy ...2B 48
Crai. Powy ...3D 47
Craig-cefn-parc. Swan ...2B 56
Craig-llwyn. Shrp ...2D 25
Craignant. Shrp ...1D 25
Craig-y-Duke. Neat ...2C 57
Craig-y-nos. Powy ...1D 57
Cranage. Ches ...1D 19
Crank. Mers ...1C 11
Craven Arms. Shrp ...3B 32
Crawford. Lanc ...1B 10
Creamore Bank. Shrp ...1C 27
Credenhill. Here ...1B 50
Cregrina. Powy ...3C 39
Creigiau. Card ...1B 64
Cressage. Shrp ...1C 33
Cresselly. Pemb ...2D 53
Cresswell Quay. Pemb ...2D 53
Crewe. Ches ...2B 18
(nr. Farndon)
Crewe. Ches ...2D 19
(nr. Nantwich)
Crewgreen. Powy ...3A 26
Cribbs Causeway. S Glo ...2C 67
Cribyn. Cdgn ...3A 36
Criccieth. Gwyn ...1D 21
Crick. Mon ...3B 60
Crickadarn. Powy ...1B 48
Crickheath. Shrp ...2D 25
Crickhowell. Powy ...1D 59
Criftins. Shrp ...1A 26
Criggion. Powy ...3D 25
Crinow. Pemb ...1A 54
Crocker's Ash. Here ...1C 61

Croeserw. Neat ...3D 57
Croes-Goch. Pemb ...2B 42
Croes Hywel. Mon ...1A 60
Croes-lan. Cdgn ...1C 45
Croesor. Gwyn ...3B 14
Croesowallt. Shrp ...2D 25
Croesyceiliog. Carm ...1D 55
Croesyceiliog. Torf ...3A 60
Croes-y-mwyalch. Newp ...3A 60
Croeswywaun. Gwyn ...2A 14
Croft. Warr ...1D 11
Crofty. Swan ...3A 56
Cromhall. S Glo ...3D 61
Cromhall Common. S Glo ...1D 67
Cronton. Mers ...2B 10
Crosby. Mers ...1A 10
Cross Ash. Mon ...1B 60
Cross Foxes. Gwyn ...3C 23
Crossgates. Powy ...2B 38
Cross Hands. Carm ...1A 56
(nr. Ammanford)
Crosshands. Carm ...3A 44
(nr. Whitland)
Cross Hill. Glos ...3C 61
Cross Houses. Shrp ...1C 33
Cross Inn. Cdgn ...2A 36
(nr. Aberaeron)
Cross Inn. Cdgn ...3C 35
(nr. New Quay)
Cross Inn. Rhon ...1B 64
Crosskeys. Cphy ...3D 59
Cross Lane Head. Shrp ...2D 33
Crosslanes. Shrp ...3A 26
Cross Lanes. Wrex ...3A 18
Cross Oak. Powy ...3C 49
Crossway. Mon ...1B 60
Crossway. Powy ...3B 38
Crossway Green. Mon ...3C 61
Crosswell. Pemb ...2A 44
Crosswood. Cdgn ...1B 36
Crow Hill. Here ...3D 51
Crowton. Ches ...3C 11
Croxton Green. Ches ...2C 19
Cruckmeore. Shrp ...1B 32
Cruckton. Shrp ...3B 26
Crudgington. Telf ...2D 27
Crug. Powy ...1C 39
Crughywel. Powy ...1D 59
Crugybar. Carm ...2B 46
Crug-y-byddar. Powy ...3C 31
Crumlin. Cphy ...3D 59
Crumpsbrook. Shrp ...1D 41
Crundale. Pemb ...1C 53
Crwbin. Carm ...1D 55
Crymych. Pemb ...2A 44
Crynant. Neat ...2C 57
Cublington. Here ...2A 50
Cuddington. Ches ...3D 11
Cuddington Heath. Ches ...3B 18
Cuerdley Cross. Warr ...2C 11
Culcheth. Warr ...1D 11
Culmington. Shrp ...3B 32
Cusop. Here ...1D 49
Cutiau. Gwyn ...3B 22
Cuttybridge. Pemb ...1C 53
Cwm. Blae ...2C 59
Cwm. Den ...3B 8
Cwm. Powy ...2D 31
Cwmafan. Neat ...3C 57
Cwmaman. Rhon ...3A 58
Cwmann. Carm ...1A 46
Cwmbach. Carm ...3B 44
Cwmbach. Powy ...2C 49
Cwmbach. Rhon ...2B 58
Cwmbach Llechryd. Powy ...3B 38
Cwmbelan. Powy ...3A 30
Cwmbran. Torf ...3D 59
Cwmbrwyno. Cdgn ...3C 29
Cwm Capel. Carm ...2D 55
Cwmcarn. Cphy ...3D 59
Cwmcarvan. Mon ...2B 60
Cwm-celyn. Blae ...2D 59
Cwmcerdinen. Swan ...2B 56
Cwm-Cewydd. Gwyn ...3D 23
Cwmcoy. Cdgn ...1B 44
Cwmcrawnon. Powy ...1C 59
Cwmcych. Pemb ...2B 44
Cwmdare. Rhon ...2A 58
Cwmdu. Carm ...2B 46
Cwmdu. Powy ...3C 49
Cwmduad. Carm ...2C 45
Cwm Dulais. Swan ...2B 56
Cwmerfyn. Cdgn ...3B 28
Cwmfelin. B'end ...1D 63
Cwmfelin Boeth. Carm ...1A 54
Cwmfelinfach. Cphy ...3C 59
Cwmfelin Mynach. Carm ...3B 44
Cwmffrwd. Carm ...1D 55
Cwmgiedd. Powy ...1C 57

Cwmgors. Neat ...1C 57
Cwmgwili. Carm ...1A 56
Cwmgwrach. Neat ...2D 57
Cwmhiraeth. Carm ...2C 45
Cwmifor. Carm ...3B 46
Cwmisfael. Carm ...1D 55
Cwm-Llinau. Powy ...1D 29
Cwmllynfell. Neat ...1C 57
Cwm-mawr. Carm ...1A 56
Cwm-miles. Carm ...3A 44
Cwmorgan. Carm ...2B 44
Cwmparc. Rhon ...3A 58
Cwm Penmachno.
  Cnwy ...3C 15
Cwmpennar. Rhon ...2B 58
Cwm Plysgog. Pemb ...1A 44
Cwmrhos. Powy ...3C 49
Cwmsychpant. Cdgn ...1D 45
Cwmsyfiog. Cphy ...2C 59
Cwmsymlog. Cdgn ...3B 28
Cwmtillery. Blae ...2D 59
Cwm-twrch Isaf. Powy ...2C 57
Cwm-twrch Uchaf.
  Powy ...1C 57
Cwmwysg. Powy ...3D 47
Cwm-y-glo. Gwyn ...1A 14
Cwmyoy. Mon ...3A 50
Cwmystwyth. Cdgn ...1C 37
Cwrt. Gwyn ...2B 28
Cwrtnewydd. Cdgn ...1D 45
Cwrt-y-Cadno. Carm ...1B 46
Cydweli. Carm ...2D 55
Cyffylliog. Den ...2B 16
Cymau. Flin ...2D 17
Cymer. Rhon ...3D 57
Cymmer. Neat ...3D 57
Cymmer. Rhon ...3B 58
Cyncoed. Card ...1C 65
Cynghordy. Carm ...2D 47
Cynghordy. Swan ...2B 56
Cynheidre. Carm ...2D 55
Cynonville. Neat ...3D 57
Cynwyd. Den ...3B 16
Cynwyl Elfed. Carm ...3C 45
Cywarch. Gwyn ...3D 23

D

Dafen. Carm ...2A 56
Dale. Pemb ...2B 52
Danesford. Shrp ...2D 33
Daren. Powy ...1D 59
Daresbury. Hal ...2C 11
Darliston. Shrp ...1C 27
Darowen. Powy ...1D 29
Davenham. Ches ...3D 11
David's Well. Powy ...3C 31
Dawley. Telf ...1D 33
Dawn. Cnwy ...3D 7
Daywall. Shrp ...1D 25
Ddol. Flin ...3C 9
Ddol Cownwy. Powy ...3B 24
Dean Park. Shrp ...2C 41
Defynnog. Powy ...3A 48
Deganwy. Cnwy ...3C 7
Deiniolen. Gwyn ...1A 14
Delamere. Ches ...1C 19
Denbigh. Den ...1B 16
Denio. Gwyn ...1C 21
Deri. Cphy ...2C 59
Derrington. Shrp ...2D 33
Derwen. Den ...2B 16
Derwen Gam. Cdgn ...3D 35
Derwenlas. Powy ...2B 28
Deuddwr. Powy ...3D 25
Devauden. Mon ...3B 60
Devil's Bridge. Cdgn ...1C 37
Dewshall Court. Here ...2B 50
Diddlebury. Shrp ...3C 33
Didley. Here ...2B 50
Dihewyd. Cdgn ...3D 35
Dilwyn. Here ...3B 40
Dinas. Carm ...2B 44
Dinas. Gwyn ...1B 20
Dinas. Pemb ...2D 43
Dinas Dinlle. Gwyn ...2D 13
Dinas Mawddwy. Gwyn ...3D 23
Dinas Powys. V Glam ...2C 65
Dinbych. Den ...1B 16
Dinbych-y-Pysgod. Pemb ...2A 54
Dinedor. Here ...2C 51
Dinedor Cross. Here ...2C 51
Dingestow. Mon ...1B 60
Dingle. Mers ...2A 10
Dinmael. Cnwy ...3B 16
Dinorwic. Gwyn ...1A 14
Discoed. Powy ...2D 39
Disserth. Powy ...3B 38

Ditton. Hal ...2B 10
Ditton Priors. Shrp ...3D 33
Dixton. Mon ...1C 61
Dobs Hill. Flin ...1A 18
Dobson's Bridge. Shrp ...1B 26
Docklow. Here ...3C 41
Doc Penfro. Pemb ...2C 53
Doddington. Shrp ...1D 41
Dodington. S Glo ...1D 67
Dodleston. Ches ...1A 18
Dolanog. Powy ...3B 24
Dolau. Powy ...2C 39
Dolau. Rhon ...1B 64
Dolbenmaen. Gwyn ...3A 14
Doley. Shrp ...2D 27
Dol-fach. Powy ...1A 30
  (nr. Llanbrynmair)
Dolfach. Powy ...1A 38
  (nr. Llanidloes)
Dolfor. Powy ...3C 31
Dolgarrog. Cnwy ...1C 15
Dolgellau. Gwyn ...3C 23
Dolgoch. Gwyn ...1B 28
Dol-gran. Carm ...2D 45
Dolhelfa. Powy ...1A 38
Dolley Green. Powy ...2D 39
Dollwen. Cdgn ...3B 28
Dolphin. Flin ...3C 9
Dolwen. Cnwy ...3D 7
Dolwyddelan. Cnwy ...2C 15
Dol-y-Bont. Cdgn ...3B 28
Dolyhir. Powy ...3D 39
Domgay. Powy ...3D 25
Donnington. Here ...2D 51
Donnington. Shrp ...1B 32
Donnington. Telf ...3D 27
Dormington. Here ...1C 51
Dorrington. Shrp ...1B 32
Dorstone. Here ...1A 50
Dotham. IOA ...3C 5
Dovaston. Shrp ...2A 26
Dowlais. Mer T ...2B 58
Downall Green. G Man ...1C 11
Downend. S Glo ...2D 67
Down, The. Shrp ...2D 33
Downton on the Rock.
  Here ...1B 40
Doynton. S Glo ...2D 67
Draethen. Cphy ...1D 65
Dreenhill. Pemb ...1C 53
Drefach. Carm ...1A 56
  (nr. Meidrim)
Drefach. Carm ...2C 45
  (nr. Newcastle Emlyn)
Drefach. Carm ...3B 44
  (nr. Tumble)
Drefach. Cdgn ...1A 46
Drope. V Glam ...2C 65
Druid. Den ...3B 16
Druidston. Pemb ...1B 52
Drury. Flin ...1D 17
Drybrook. Glos ...1C 61
Drybrook. Here ...1C 61
Dryslwyn. Carm ...3A 46
Dryton. Shrp ...1C 33
Duckington. Ches ...2B 18
Duddon. Ches ...1C 19
Dudleston. Shrp ...1A 26
Dudleston Heath. Shrp ...1A 26
Dudston. Shrp ...2D 31
Dudwells. Pemb ...1C 53
Duffryn. Neat ...3D 57
Dukestown. Blae ...1C 59
Dulas. IOA ...2D 5
Dundry. N Som ...3C 67
Dunham-on-the-Hill. Ches ...3B 10
Dunham Town. G Man ...2D 11
Dunham Woodhouses.
  G Man ...2D 11
Dunkerton. Bath ...3D 67
Dunvant. Swan ...3A 56
Durlow Common. Here ...2D 51
Dursley. Glos ...3D 61
Dursley Cross. Glos ...1D 61
Dutlas. Powy ...1D 39
Dutton. Ches ...3C 11
Dwygyfylchi. Cnwy ...3C 7
Dwyran. IOA ...1D 13
Dyffryn. B'end ...3D 57
Dyffryn. Carm ...3C 45
Dyffryn. IOA ...3B 4
Dyffryn. Pemb ...2C 43
Dyffryn. V Glam ...2B 64
Dyffryn Ardudwy. Gwyn ...2A 22
Dyffryn Castell. Cdgn ...3C 29
Dyffryn Ceidrych. Carm ...3C 47
Dyffryn Cellwen. Neat ...1D 57
Dyfnant. Powy ...2D 29
Dylife. Powy ...2B 30
Dymock. Glos ...2D 51

Dyrham. *S Glo* 2D **67**
Dyserth. *Den* 3B **8**

E

Eardington. *Shrp* 2D **33**
Eardisland. *Here* 3B **40**
Eardisley. *Here* 1A **50**
Eardiston. *Shrp* 2A **26**
Eardiston. *Worc* 2D **41**
Earlestown. *Mers* 1C **11**
Earlswood. *Mon* 3B **60**
Earthcott Green. *S Glo* 1D **67**
East Aberthaw. *V Glam* 3B **64**
East Clevedon. *N Som* 2B **66**
East Dean. *Glos* 3D **51**
East Dundry. *N Som* 3C **67**
East End. *N Som* 3B **66**
Easter Compton. *S Glo* 1C **67**
Eastham. *Mers* 2A **10**
Eastham. *Worc* 2D **41**
Eastham Ferry. *Mers* 2A **10**
Easthampton. *Here* 2B **40**
Easthope. *Shrp* 2C **33**
Eastnor. *Here* 2D **51**
Easton-in-Gordano. *N Som* 2C **67**
East Wall. *Shrp* 2C **33**
East Williamston. *Pemb* 2D **53**
Eaton. *Ches* 1C **19**
Eaton. *Shrp* 3A **32**
(nr. Bishop's Castle)
Eaton. *Shrp* 2C **33**
(nr. Church Stretton)
Eaton Bishop. *Here* 2B **50**
Eaton Constantine. *Shrp* 1C **33**
Eaton upon Tern. *Shrp* 2D **27**
Ebbw Vale. *Blae* 2C **59**
Ebnal. *Ches* 3B **18**
Eccles Green. *Here* 1A **50**
Eccleston. *Ches* 1B **18**
Eccleston. *Mers* 1B **10**
Edern. *Gwyn* 1B **20**
Edge. *Shrp* 1A **32**
Edgebolton. *Shrp* 2C **27**
Edge End. *Glos* 1C **61**
Edge Green. *Ches* 2B **18**
Edgeley. *Shrp* 3C **19**
Edgmond. *Telf* 3D **27**
Edgmond Marsh. *Telf* 2D **27**
Edgton. *Shrp* 3A **32**
Edstaston. *Shrp* 1C **27**
Edwardsville. *Mer T* 3B **58**
Edwinsford. *Carm* 2B **46**
Edwyn Ralph. *Here* 3D **41**
Efail-fach. *Neat* 3C **57**
Efail Isaf. *Rhon* 1B **64**
Efailnewydd. *Gwyn* 1C **21**
Efail-rhyd. *Powy* 2C **25**
Efailwen. *Carm* 3A **44**
Efenechtyd. *Den* 2C **17**
Eglwysbach. *Cnwy* 3D **7**
Eglwys Brewis. *V Glam* 3B **64**
Eglwys Fach. *Cdgn* 2B **28**
Eglwyswrw. *Pemb* 2A **44**
Egremont. *Mers* 1A **10**
Eisingrug. *Gwyn* 1B **22**
Elan Village. *Powy* 2A **38**
Elberton. *S Glo* 1D **67**
Ellerdine. *Telf* 2D **27**
Ellerdine Heath. *Telf* 2D **27**
Ellerton. *Shrp* 2D **27**
Ellesmere. *Shrp* 1B **26**
Ellesmere Port. *Ches* 3B **10**
Ellwood. *Glos* 2C **61**
Elton. *Ches* 3B **10**
Elton. *Glos* 1D **61**
Elton. *Here* 1B **40**
Elton Green. *Ches* 3B **10**
Elworth. *Ches* 1D **19**
Ely. *Card* 2C **65**
Enchmarsh. *Shrp* 2C **33**
Engine Common. *S Glo* 1D **67**
Engleseabrook. *Ches* 2D **19**
English Bicknor. *Glos* 1C **61**
Englishcombe. *Bath* 3D **67**
English Frankton. *Shrp* 2B **26**
Ensdon. *Shrp* 3A **26**
Erbistock. *Wrex* 3A **18**
Erwood. *Powy* 1B **48**
Eryrys. *Den* 2D **17**
Esgair. *Carm* 3C **45**
(nr. Carmarthen)
Esgair. *Carm* 1B **54**
(nr. St Clears)
Esgairgeiliog. *Powy* 1C **29**
Etloe. *Glos* 2D **61**
Ettiley Heath. *Ches* 1D **19**
Eudon Burnell. *Shrp* 3D **33**

Eudon George. *Shrp* 3D **33**
Evanstown. *B'end* 1A **64**
Evendine. *Here* 1D **51**
Evenjobb. *Powy* 2D **39**
Everton. *Mers* 1A **10**
Evesbatch. *Here* 1D **51**
Ewdness. *Shrp* 2D **33**
Ewenny. *V Glam* 2A **64**
Ewlo. *Flin* 1A **18**
Ewloe. *Flin* 1A **18**
Ewyas Harold. *Here* 3A **50**
Exfords Green. *Shrp* 1B **32**
Eye. *Here* 2B **40**
Eyton. *Here* 2B **40**
Eyton. *Shrp* 3A **32**
(nr. Bishop's Castle)
Eyton. *Shrp* 3A **26**
(nr. Shrewsbury)
Eyton. *Wrex* 3A **18**
Eyton on Severn. *Shrp* 1C **33**
Eyton upon the Weald Moors.
Telf 3D **27**

F

Faddiley. *Ches* 2C **19**
Fagwyr. *Swan* 2B **56**
Failand. *N Som* 2C **67**
Fairbourne. *Gwyn* 3B **22**
Fairwater. *Card* 2C **65**
Falcon. *Here* 2D **51**
Falfield. *S Glo* 3D **61**
Far Forest. *Worc* 1D **41**
Farleigh. *N Som* 3B **66**
Farley. *N Som* 2B **66**
Farley. *Shrp* 1A **32**
(nr. Shrewsbury)
Farley. *Shrp* 1D **33**
(nr. Telford)
Farlow. *Shrp* 3D **33**
Farmborough. *Bath* 3D **67**
Far Moor. *G Man* 1C **11**
Farndon. *Ches* 2B **18**
Farnworth. *Hal* 2C **11**
Fauls. *Shrp* 1C **27**
Fawley Chapel. *Here* 3C **51**
Fazakerley. *Mers* 1A **10**
Fearnhead. *Warr* 1D **11**
Felhampton. *Shrp* 3B **32**
Felindre. *Carm* 3A **46**
(nr. Llandeilo)
Felindre. *Carm* 2B **46**
(nr. Llandovery)
Felindre. *Carm* 2C **45**
(nr. Newcastle Emlyn)
Felindre. *Powy* 3C **31**
Felindre. *Powy* 2B **56**
Felindre Farchog. *Pemb* 2A **44**
Felinfach. *Cdgn* 3A **36**
Felinfach. *Powy* 2B **48**
Felinfoel. *Carm* 2A **56**
Felingwmisaf. *Carm* 3A **46**
Felingwmuchaf. *Carm* 3A **46**
Felin Newydd. *Powy* 1B **30**
(nr. Newtown)
Felin Newydd. *Powy* 2D **25**
(nr. Oswestry)
Felin Wnda. *Cdgn* 1C **45**
Felinwynt. *Cdgn* 3B **34**
Felton. *Here* 1C **51**
Felton. *N Som* 3C **67**
Felton Butler. *Shrp* 3A **26**
Fenn's Bank. *Wrex* 1C **27**
Ferndale. *Rhon* 3A **58**
Ferryside. *Carm* 1C **55**
Ffairfach. *Carm* 3B **46**
Ffair Rhos. *Cdgn* 2C **37**
Ffaldybrenin. *Carm* 1B **46**
Ffarmers. *Carm* 1B **46**
Ffawyddog. *Powy* 1D **59**
Ffodun. *Powy* 1D **31**
Ffont-y-gari. *V Glam* 3B **64**
Fforest. *Carm* 2A **56**
Fforest-fach. *Swan* 3B **56**
Fforest Goch. *Neat* 2C **57**
Ffostrasol. *Cdgn* 1C **45**
Ffos-y-ffin. *Cdgn* 2D **35**
Ffrith. *Flin* 2D **17**
Ffrwdgrech. *Powy* 3B **48**
Ffynnon-ddrain. *Carm* 3D **45**
Ffynnongroyw. *Flin* 2C **9**
Ffynnon Gynydd. *Powy* 1C **49**
Ffynnonoer. *Cdgn* 3A **36**
Filton. *Bris* 2D **67**
Fishguard. *Pemb* 2C **43**
Fishponds. *Bris* 2D **67**
Fishpool. *Glos* 3D **51**
Fishpools. *Powy* 2C **39**

Fitz. *Shrp* 3B **26**
Five Bridges. *Here* 1D **51**
Five Roads. *Carm* 2D **55**
Flax Bourton. *N Som* 3C **67**
Flaxley. *Glos* 1D **61**
Flemingston. *V Glam* 2B **64**
Flint. *Flin* 3D **9**
Flint Mountain. *Flin* 3D **9**
Flintsham. *Here* 3A **40**
Flixton. *G Man* 1D **11**
Fochriw. *Cphy* 2C **59**
Foel. *Powy* 3A **24**
Font-y-gary. *V Glam* 3B **64**
Ford. *Shrp* 3B **26**
Forden. *Powy* 1D **31**
Ford Heath. *Shrp* 3B **26**
Forge. *Powy* 2C **29**
Forge Side. *Torf* 2D **59**
Forge, The. *Here* 3A **40**
Forthay. *Glos* 3D **61**
Forton. *Shrp* 3B **26**
Forton. *Staf* 2D **27**
Forton Heath. *Shrp* 3B **26**
Four Alls, The. *Shrp* 1D **27**
Four Crosses. *Powy* 1B **30**
(nr. Llanerfyl)
Four Crosses. *Powy* 3D **25**
(nr. Llanymynech)
Four Mile Bridge. *IOA* 3B **4**
Four Oaks. *Glos* 3D **51**
Four Roads. *Carm* 2D **55**
Fowley Common. *Warr* 1D **11**
Fownhope. *Here* 2C **51**
Foxwist Green. *Ches* 1D **19**
Foxwood. *Shrp* 1D **41**
Foy. *Here* 3C **51**
Frampton Cotterell. *S Glo* 1D **67**
Frampton on Severn.
Glos 2D **61**
Frandley. *Ches* 3D **11**
Frankby. *Mers* 2D **9**
Frank's Bridge. *Powy* 3C **39**
Frankwell. *Shrp* 3B **26**
Freshwater East. *Pemb* 3D **53**
Fretherne. *Glos* 2D **61**
Freystrop. *Pemb* 1C **53**
Friog. *Gwyn* 3B **22**
Frith Common. *Worc* 2D **41**
Frochas. *Powy* 1C **31**
Frodesley. *Shrp* 1C **33**
Frodsham. *Ches* 3C **11**
Fromes Hill. *Here* 1D **51**
Fron. *Carm* 2C **47**
Fron. *Gwyn* 2A **14**
(nr. Caernarfon)
Fron. *Gwyn* 1C **21**
(nr. Pwllheli)
Fron. *Powy* 2B **38**
(nr. Llandrindod Wells)
Fron. *Powy* 2C **31**
(nr. Newtown)
Fron. *Powy* 1D **31**
(nr. Welshpool)
Froncysyllte. *Den* 3D **17**
Frongoch. *Gwyn* 1A **24**
Fron Isaf. *Wrex* 3D **17**
Fronoleu. *Gwyn* 1C **23**
Fuller's Moor. *Ches* 2B **18**
Furnace. *Carm* 2A **56**
Furnace. *Cdgn* 2B **28**

G

Gadfa. *IOA* 2D **5**
Gaer. *Powy* 3C **49**
Gaerwen. *IOA* 3D **5**
Gallt Melyd. *Den* 2B **8**
Ganarew. *Here* 1C **61**
Ganllwyd. *Gwyn* 2C **23**
Garden City. *Flin* 1A **18**
Garden Village. *Swan* 3A **56**
Garmston. *Shrp* 1D **33**
Garnant. *Carm* 1B **56**
Garndiffaith. *Torf* 2D **59**
Garndolbenmaen. *Gwyn* 3D **13**
Garnfadryn. *Gwyn* 1B **20**
Garnlydan. *Blae* 1C **59**
Garnswllt. *Swan* 2B **56**
Garn-yr-erw. *Torf* 1D **59**
Garreg. *Gwyn* 3B **14**
Garston. *Mers* 2B **10**
Garswood. *Mers* 1C **11**
Garth. *B'end* 3D **57**
Garth. *Cdgn* 3B **28**
Garth. *Den* 3D **17**
Garth. *Gwyn* 1A **22**
Garth. *Powy* 1A **48**
(nr. Builth Wells)

Garth. *Powy* 1D **39**
(nr. Knighton)
Garthbrengy. *Powy* 2B **48**
Gartheli. *Cdgn* 3A **36**
Garthmyl. *Powy* 2C **31**
Garth Owen. *Powy* 2C **31**
Garway. *Here* 3B **50**
Garway Common. *Here* 3B **50**
Garway Hill. *Here* 3B **50**
Gateacre. *Mers* 2B **10**
Gatesheath. *Ches* 1B **18**
Gaufron. *Powy* 2A **38**
Gaunt's Earthcott.
S Glo .1D **67**
Gayton. *Mers* 2D **9**
Gell. *Cnwy* 1D **15**
Gelli. *Pemb* 1D **53**
Gelli. *Rhon* 3A **58**
Gellifor. *Den* 1C **17**
Gelligaer. *Cphy* 3C **59**
Gellilydan. *Gwyn* 1B **22**
Gellinudd. *Neat* 2C **57**
Gellywen. *Carm* 3B **44**
Geneva. *Cdgn* 3D **35**
Georgetown. *Blae* 2C **59**
Gerlan. *Gwyn* 1B **14**
Gethsemane. *Pemb* 1D **43**
Geuffordd. *Powy* 3D **25**
Gignog. *Pemb* 3B **42**
Gileston. *V Glam* 3B **64**
Gilfach. *Cphy* 3C **59**
Gilfach Goch. *Rhon* 3A **58**
Gilfachreda. *Cdgn* 3D **35**
Gillar's Green. *Mers* 1B **10**
Gilwern. *Mon* 1D **59**
Gladestry. *Powy* 3D **39**
Glais. *Swan* 2C **57**
Glanaman. *Carm* 1B **56**
Glan-Conwy. *Cnwy* 2D **15**
Glan Duar. *Carm* 1A **46**
Glandwr. *Blae* 2D **59**
Glandwr. *Pemb* 3A **44**
Glan-Dwyfach. *Gwyn* 3D **13**
Glandy Cross. *Carm* 3A **44**
Glandyfi. *Cdgn* 2B **28**
Glangrwyney. *Powy* 1D **59**
Glanmule. *Powy* 2C **31**
Glanrhyd. *Gwyn* 1B **20**
Glan-rhyd. *Neat* 2C **57**
Glanrhyd. *Pemb* 1A **44**
(nr. Cardigan)
Glan-rhyd. *Pemb* 2A **44**
(nr. Crymmych)
Glan-y-don. *Flin* 3C **9**
Glan-y-nant. *Powy* 3A **30**
Glan-yr-afon. *Gwyn* 3B **16**
Glan-yr-afon. *IOA* 2B **6**
Glan-yr-afon. *Powy* 1B **30**
Glan-y-wern. *Gwyn* 1B **22**
Glasbury. *Powy* 2C **49**
Glascoed. *Den* 3A **8**
Glascoed. *Mon* 2A **60**
Glascwm. *Powy* 3C **39**
Glasfryn. *Cnwy* 2A **16**
Glasinfryn. *Gwyn* 1A **14**
Glaspwll. *Powy* 2C **29**
Glasshouse. *Glos* 3D **51**
Glazebrook. *Warr* 1D **11**
Glazebury. *Warr* 1D **11**
Glazeley. *Shrp* 3D **33**
Gledrid. *Shrp* 1D **25**
Gleiniant. *Powy* 2A **30**
Glewstone. *Here* 3C **51**
Glyn. *Cnwy* 3D **7**
Glynarthen. *Cdgn* 1C **45**
Glynbrochan. *Powy* 3A **30**
Glyn Ceiriog. *Wrex* 1D **25**
Glyncoch. *Rhon* 3B **58**
Glyncorrwg. *Neat* 3D **57**
Glyndyfrdwy. *Den* 3C **17**
Glyn Ebwy. *Blae* 2C **59**
Glynllan. *B'end* 1A **64**
Glyn-neath. *Neat* 2D **57**
Glynogwr. *B'end* 1A **64**
Glyntaff. *Rhon* 1B **64**
Glyntawe. *Powy* 1D **57**
Glynteg. *Carm* 2C **45**
Gobowen. *Shrp* 1A **26**
Godre'r-graig. *Neat* 2C **57**
Goetre. *Mon* 2A **60**
Goginan. *Cdgn* 3B **28**
Golan. *Gwyn* 3A **14**
Golborne. *G Man* 1D **11**
Goldcliff. *Newp* 1A **66**
Golden Grove. *Carm* 1A **56**
Golden Hill. *Pemb* 3C **43**
Golding. *Shrp* 1C **33**
Goldstone. *Shrp* 2D **27**
Golfa. *Powy* 2C **25**

Goodrich. *Here* 1C **61**
Goodwick. *Pemb* 2C **43**
Goose Green. *S Glo* 1D **67**
Gors. *Cdgn* 1B **36**
Gorsedd. *Flin* 3C **9**
Gorseinon. *Swan* 3A **56**
Gorsgoch. *Cdgn* 3D **35**
Gorslas. *Carm* 1A **56**
Gorsley. *Glos* 3D **51**
Gorsley Common. *Here* 3D **51**
Gorstella. *Ches* 1A **18**
Gorsty Common. *Here* 2B **50**
Gossington. *Glos* 2D **61**
Govilon. *Mon* 1D **59**
Gowerton. *Swan* 3A **56**
Goytre. *Neat* 1C **63**
Grafton. *Here* 2B **50**
Grafton. *Shrp* 3B **26**
Grafton. *Worc* 2C **41**
Graianrhyd. *Den* 2D **17**
Graig. *Carm* 2D **55**
Graig. *Cnwy* 3D **7**
Graig. *Den* .3B **8**
Graig-fechan. *Den* 2C **17**
Graig Penllyn. *V Glam* 2A **64**
Grange. *Here* 1B **40**
Grange. *Mers* 2D **9**
Grangetown. *Card* 2C **65**
Granston. *Pemb* 2B **42**
Grappenhall. *Warr* 2D **11**
Grassendale. *Mers* 2A **10**
Gravelhill. *Shrp* 3B **26**
Greasby. *Mers* 2D **9**
Great Barrow. *Ches* 1B **18**
Great Bolas. *Telf* 2D **27**
Great Budworth. *Ches* 3D **11**
Great Crosby. *Mers* 1A **10**
Great Doward. *Here* 1C **61**
Great Lyth. *Shrp* 1B **32**
Great Ness. *Shrp* 3B **26**
Great Oak. *Mon* 2A **60**
Great Ryton. *Shrp* 1B **32**
Great Sankey. *Warr* 2C **11**
Great Sutton. *Ches* 3A **10**
Great Sutton. *Shrp* 3C **33**
Great Wytheford. *Shrp* 3C **27**
Greenfield. *Flin* 3C **9**
Green Lane. *Shrp* 2D **27**
Greenway. *Pemb* 3D **43**
Greenway. *V Glam* 2B **64**
Greete. *Shrp* 1C **41**
Grendon Green. *Here* 3C **41**
Gresford. *Wrex* 2A **18**
Gretton. *Shrp* 2C **33**
Griffithstown. *Torf* 3D **59**
Grimpo. *Shrp* 2A **26**
Grindle. *Shrp* 1D **33**
Grindley Brook. *Shrp* 3C **19**
Grinshill. *Shrp* 2C **27**
Groes. *Cnwy* 1B **16**
Groes. *Neat* 1C **63**
Groes-faen. *Rhon* 1B **64**
Groesffordd. *Gwyn* 1B **20**
Groesffordd. *Powy* 3B **48**
Groeslon. *Gwyn* 2D **13**
Groes-lwyd. *Powy* 3D **25**
Groes-wen. *Cphy* 1C **65**
Gronant. *Flin* 2B **8**
Grosmont. *Mon* 3B **50**
Grovesend. *Swan* 2A **56**
Guilden Down. *Shrp* 3A **32**
Guilden Sutton. *Ches* 1B **18**
Guilsfield. *Powy* 3D **25**
Gumfreston. *Pemb* 2A **54**
Gurnos. *Powy* 1C **57**
Gwaelod-y-garth. *Card* 1C **65**
Gwaenynog Bach. *Den* 1B **16**
Gwaenysgor. *Flin* 2B **8**
Gwalchmai. *IOA* 3C **5**
Gwastad. *Pemb* 3D **43**
Gwaun-Cae-Gurwen.
  Neat 1C **57**
Gwaun-y-bara. *Cphy* 1C **65**
Gwbert. *Cdgn* 3A **34**
Gwehelog. *Mon* 2A **60**
Gwenddwr. *Powy* 1B **48**
Gwernaffield. *Flin* 1D **17**
Gwernesney. *Mon* 2B **60**
Gwernogle. *Carm* 2A **46**
Gwern-y-go. *Powy* 2D **31**
Gwernymynydd. *Flin* 1D **17**
Gwersyllt. *Wrex* 2A **18**
Gwespyr. *Flin* 2C **9**
Gwredog. *IOA* 2D **5**
Gwyddelwern. *Den* 3B **16**
Gwyddgrug. *Carm* 2D **45**
Gwynfryn. *Wrex* 2D **17**
Gwystre. *Powy* 2B **38**
Gwytherin. *Cnwy* 1D **15**

Gyfelia. *Wrex* 3A **18**
Gyffin. *Cnwy* 3C **7**

H

Habberley. *Shrp* 1A **32**
Hadley. *Telf* 3D **27**
Hadnall. *Shrp* 2C **27**
Hagley. *Here* 1C **51**
Hakin. *Pemb* 2B **52**
Hale. *Hal* .2B **10**
Hale Bank. *Hal* 2B **10**
Hales. *Staf* 1D **27**
Halewood. *Mers* 2B **10**
Halford. *Shrp* 3B **32**
Halfpenny Furze. *Carm* 1B **54**
Halfway. *Carm* 2B **46**
Halfway. *Powy* 2D **47**
Halfway House. *Shrp* 3A **26**
Halkyn. *Flin* 3D **9**
Hallatrow. *Bath* 3D **67**
Hallen. *S Glo* 1C **67**
Hallowsgate. *Ches* 1C **19**
Hallwood Green. *Glos* 2D **51**
Halmond's Frome. *Here* 1D **51**
Halmore. *Glos* 2D **61**
Halton. *Hal* 2C **11**
Halton. *Wrex* 1A **26**
Ham. *Glos* 3D **61**
Hambrook. *S Glo* 2D **67**
Ham Green. *Here* 1D **51**
Ham Green. *N Som* 2C **67**
Hamperley. *Shrp* 3B **32**
Hampton. *Shrp* 3D **33**
Hampton Bishop. *Here* 2C **51**
Hampton Heath. *Ches* 3C **19**
Hampton Loade. *Shrp* 3D **33**
Handbridge. *Ches* 1B **18**
Handley. *Ches* 2B **18**
Hanham. *S Glo* 2D **67**
Hanham Green. *S Glo* 2D **67**
Hankelow. *Ches* 3D **19**
Hanley Childe. *Worc* 2D **41**
Hanley William. *Worc* 2D **41**
Hanmer. *Wrex* 1B **26**
Hanwood. *Shrp* 1B **32**
Hapsford. *Ches* 3B **10**
Hardwick. *Shrp* 2A **32**
Hardwicke. *Here* 1D **49**
Haresfinch. *Mers* 1C **11**
Harewood End. *Here* 3C **51**
Hargrave. *Ches* 1B **18**
Harlech. *Gwyn* 1A **22**
Harlescott. *Shrp* 3C **27**
Harley. *Shrp* 1C **33**
Harmer Hill. *Shrp* 2B **26**
Harnage. *Shrp* 1C **33**
Haroldston West. *Pemb* 1B **52**
Harpley. *Worc* 2D **41**
Harry Stoke. *S Glo* 2D **67**
Hartford. *Ches* 3D **11**
Harthill. *Ches* 2C **19**
Harton. *Shrp* 3B **32**
Hasguard. *Pemb* 2B **52**
Haslington. *Ches* 2D **19**
Hassall. *Ches* 2C **27**
Hatchmere. *Ches* 3C **11**
Hatfield. *Here* 3C **41**
Hatherton. *Ches* 3D **19**
Hatton. *Shrp* 2B **32**
Hatton. *Warr* 2C **11**
Hatton Heath. *Ches* 1B **18**
Haughton. *Shrp* 2D **33**
  (nr. Bridgnorth)
Haughton. *Shrp* 2A **26**
  (nr. Oswestry)
Haughton. *Shrp* 1D **33**
  (nr. Shifnal)
Haughton. *Shrp* 3C **27**
  (nr. Shrewsbury)
Haughton Moss. *Ches* 2C **19**
Haven. *Here* 3B **40**
Haverfordwest. *Pemb* 1C **53**
Hawarden. *Flin* 1A **18**
Hawen. *Cdgn* 1C **45**
Haybridge. *Shrp* 1D **41**
Haydock. *Mers* 1C **11**
Hay-on-Wye. *Powy* 1D **49**
Hayscastle. *Pemb* 3B **42**
Hayscastle Cross. *Pemb* 3C **43**
Hayton's Bent. *Shrp* 3C **33**
Hazler. *Shrp* 2B **32**
Headley Park. *Bris* 3C **67**
Heartsease. *Powy* 2C **39**
Heatley. *G Man* 2D **11**
Hebden Green. *Ches* 1D **19**
Hebron. *Carm* 3A **44**

Hegdon Hill. *Here* 3C **41**
Helsby. *Ches* 3B **10**
Helygain. *Flin* 3D **9**
Hem, The. *Shrp* 1D **33**
Henallt. *Carm* 3D **45**
Henbury. *Bris* 2C **67**
Hendomen. *Powy* 2D **31**
Hendre. *B'end* 1A **64**
Hendreforgan. *Rhon* 3C **63**
Hendy. *Carm* 2A **56**
Heneglwys. *IOA* 3D **5**
Henfeddau Fawr. *Pemb* 2B **44**
Henfield. *S Glo* 2D **67**
Hengoed. *Cphy* 3C **59**
Hengoed. *Shrp* 1D **25**
Heniarth. *Powy* 1C **31**
Henley. *Shrp* 3B **32**
  (nr. Church Stretton)
Henley. *Shrp* 1C **41**
  (nr. Ludlow)
Henllan. *Cdgn* 1C **45**
Henllan. *Den* 1B **16**
Henllan. *Mon* 3D **49**
Henllan Amgoed. *Carm* 3A **44**
Henllys. *Torf* 3D **59**
Henryd. *Cnwy* 3C **7**
Henry's Moat. *Pemb* 3D **43**
Heol Senni. *Powy* 3A **48**
Heol-y-Cyw. *B'end* 1A **64**
Herbrandston. *Pemb* 2B **52**
Hereford. *Here* 2C **51**
Hermon. *Carm* 3B **46**
  (nr. Llandeilo)
Hermon. *Carm* 2C **45**
  (nr. Newcastle Emlyn)
Hermon. *IOA* 1C **13**
Hermon. *Pemb* 2B **44**
Heswall. *Mers* 2D **9**
Hewelsfield. *Glos* 2C **61**
Hewish. *N Som* 3A **66**
Heyop. *Powy* 1D **39**
Higford. *Shrp* 1D **33**
High Ercall. *Telf* 3C **27**
Higher End. *G Man* 1C **11**
Higher Kinnerton. *Flin* 1A **18**
Higher Shotton. *Flin* 1A **18**
Higher Shurlach. *Ches* 3D **11**
Higher Walton. *Warr* 2D **11**
Higher Whitley. *Ches* 3D **11**
Higher Wincham. *Ches* 3D **11**
Higher Wych. *Ches* 3B **18**
Highgate. *Powy* 2C **31**
High Green. *Shrp* 3D **33**
High Hatton. *Shrp* 2D **27**
Highlands, The. *Shrp* 3D **33**
High Lane. *Shrp* 2D **41**
High Legh. *Ches* 2D **11**
Highley. *Shrp* 3D **33**
High Littleton. *Bath* 3D **67**
Highmoor Hill. *Mon* 1B **66**
Hightown. *Mers* 1D **9**
Highway. *Here* 1B **50**
Highwood. *Worc* 2D **41**
Hill. *S Glo* 3D **61**
Hillend. *Swan* 3D **55**
Hillersland. *Glos* 1C **61**
Hill Gate. *Here* 3B **50**
Hillside. *Shrp* 3D **33**
Hillside. *Worc* 2D **41**
Hindford. *Shrp* 1A **26**
Hindley Green. *G Man* 1D **11**
Hinstock. *Shrp* 2D **27**
Hinton. *Here* 2A **50**
Hinton. *Shrp* 1B **32**
Hinton. *S Glo* 2D **67**
Hinton Blewett. *Bath* 3C **67**
Hints. *Shrp* 1D **41**
Hiraeth. *Carm* 3A **44**
Hirnant. *Powy* 2B **24**
Hirwaen. *Den* 1C **17**
Hirwaun. *Rhon* 2A **58**
Hoarwithy. *Here* 3C **51**
Hobarris. *Shrp* 1A **40**
Hodgeston. *Pemb* 3D **53**
Hodley. *Powy* 2C **31**
Hodnet. *Shrp* 2D **27**
Holdgate. *Shrp* 3C **33**
Hollinfare. *Warr* 1D **11**
Hollinswood. *Telf* 1D **33**
Hollinwood. *Shrp* 2C **27**
Hollybush. *Cphy* 2C **59**
Hollyhurst. *Ches* 3C **19**
Holme Lacy. *Here* 2C **51**
Holme Marsh. *Here* 3A **40**
Holmer. *Here* 1C **51**
Holt. *Wrex* 2B **18**
Holyhead. *IOA* 2B **4**
Holywell. *Flin* 3C **9**
Homer. *Shrp* 1D **33**

Homer Green. *Mers* 1A **10**
Hom Green. *Here* 3C **51**
Honeyborough. *Pemb* 2C **53**
Honnington. *Telf* 3D **27**
Hook. *Pemb* 1C **53**
Hook-a-Gate. *Shrp* 1B **32**
Hookgate. *Staf* 1D **27**
Hook Street. *Glos* 3D **61**
Hoole. *Ches* 1B **18**
Hooton. *Ches* 3A **10**
Hope. *Flin* 2A **18**
Hope. *Powy* 1D **31**
Hope. *Shrp* 1A **32**
Hope Bagot. *Shrp* 1C **41**
Hope Bowdler. *Shrp* 2B **32**
Hope Mansell. *Here* 1D **61**
Hopesay. *Shrp* 3A **32**
Hope under Dinmore. *Here* 3C **41**
Hopley's Green. *Here* 3A **40**
Hopton. *Powy* 2D **31**
Hopton. *Shrp* 2A **26**
  (nr. Oswestry)
Hopton. *Shrp* 2C **27**
  (nr. Wem)
Hopton Cangeford. *Shrp* 3C **33**
Hopton Castle. *Shrp* 1A **40**
Hoptonheath. *Shrp* 1A **40**
Hopton Wafers. *Shrp* 1D **41**
Horderley. *Shrp* 3B **32**
Hordley. *Shrp* 1A **26**
Horeb. *Carm* 3A **46**
  (nr. Brechfa)
Horeb. *Carm* 2D **55**
  (nr. Llanelli)
Horeb. *Cdgn* 1C **45**
Horfield. *Bris* 2D **67**
Horsecastle. *N Som* 3B **66**
Horsehay. *Telf* 1D **33**
Horseman's Green. *Wrex* 3B **18**
Horsham. *Worc* 3D **41**
Horton. *Shrp* 1B **26**
Horton. *Swan* 1A **62**
Horton Green. *Ches* 3B **18**
Hortonwood. *Telf* 3D **27**
Hough. *Ches* 2D **19**
Hough Green. *Hal* 2B **10**
Houghton. *Pemb* 2C **53**
How Caple. *Here* 2D **51**
Howey. *Powy* 3B **38**
Howle. *Telf* 2D **27**
Howle Hill. *Here* 3D **51**
Howley. *Warr* 2D **11**
Howton. *Here* 3B **50**
Hoylake. *Mers* 2D **9**
Hubberston. *Pemb* 2B **52**
Hughley. *Shrp* 2C **33**
Humber Court. *Here* 3C **41**
Hundleton. *Pemb* 2C **53**
Hundred House. *Powy* 3C **39**
Hundred, The. *Here* 2C **41**
Hungerford. *Shrp* 3C **33**
Hungryhatton. *Shrp* 2D **27**
Hunstrete. *Bath* 3D **67**
Huntingdon. *Ches* 1B **18**
Huntington. *Here* 3D **39**
Huntington. *Telf* 1D **33**
Huntley. *Glos* 1D **61**
Hunt's Cross. *Mers* 2B **10**
Huntstrete. *Bath* 3D **67**
Hurdley. *Powy* 2D **31**
Hurst Green. *Ches* 3C **19**
Hurstley. *Here* 1A **50**
Hurstway Common. *Here* 1D **49**
Hutton. *N Som* 3A **66**
Huxley. *Ches* 1C **19**
Huyton. *Mers* 1B **10**
Hwlffordd. *Pemb* 1C **53**
Hyssington. *Powy* 2A **32**

I

Icelton. *N Som* 3A **66**
Idole. *Carm* 1D **55**
Ifton Heath. *Shrp* 1A **26**
Ightfield. *Shrp* 1C **27**
Ilston. *Swan* 3A **56**
Ince. *Ches* 3B **10**
Ince Blundell. *Mers* 1A **10**
Inglesbatch. *Bath* 3D **67**
Ingst. *S Glo* 1C **67**
Irby. *Mers* 2D **9**
Irlam. *G Man* 1D **11**
Iron Acton. *S Glo* 1D **67**
Ironbridge. *Telf* 1D **33**
Islington. *Telf* 2D **27**
Islwyn. *Cphy* 3D **59**
Itchington. *S Glo* 1D **67**
Itton Common. *Mon* 3B **60**

Ivington. *Here* 3B **33**
Ivington Green. *Here* 3B **40**

J

Jackfield. *Shrp* 1D **33**
Jameston. *Pemb* 3D **53**
Jeffreyston. *Pemb* 2D **53**
Jersey Marine. *Neat* 3C **57**
Jingle Street. *Mon* 1B **60**
Johnston. *Pemb* 1C **53**
Johnstown. *Carm* 1C **55**
Johnstown. *Wrex* 3A **18**
Jordanston. *Pemb* 2C **43**

K

Keckwick. *Hal* 2C **11**
Keeston. *Pemb* 1C **53**
Kelsall. *Ches* 1C **19**
Kelsterton. *Flin* 3D **9**
Kelston. *Bath* 3D **67**
Kemberton. *Shrp* 1D **33**
Kemeys Commander. *Mon* 2A **60**
Kempley. *Glos* 3D **51**
Kempley Green. *Glos* 3D **51**
Kempton. *Shrp* 3A **32**
Kenchester. *Here* 1B **50**
Kendleshire. *S Glo* 2D **67**
Kenfig. *B'end* 1D **63**
Kenfig Hill. *B'end* 1D **63**
Kenley. *Shrp* 1C **33**
Kenn. *N Som* 3B **66**
Kenstone. *Shrp* 2C **27**
Kentchurch. *Here* 3B **50**
Kent's Green. *Glos* 3D **51**
Kenwick. *Shrp* 1B **26**
Kenyon. *Warr* 1D **11**
Kerne Bridge. *Here* 1C **61**
Kerry. *Powy* 3C **31**
Kerry's Gate. *Here* 2A **50**
Kewstoke. *N Som* 3A **66**
Keynsham. *Bath* 3D **67**
Kidnal. *Ches* 3B **18**
Kidwelly. *Carm* 2D **55**
Kilcot. *Glos* 3D **51**
Kilgetty. *Pemb* 2A **54**
Killay. *Swan* 3B **56**
Kiln Green. *Here* 1C **61**
Kilpeck. *Here* 2B **50**
Kimbolton. *Here* 2C **41**
Kingcoed. *Mon* 2B **60**
King's Acre. *Here* 1B **50**
Kings Caple. *Here* 3C **51**
Kingsland. *Here* 2B **40**
Kingsland. *IOA* 2B **4**
Kingsley. *Ches* 3C **11**
Kings Moss. *Mers* 1C **11**
King's Pyon. *Here* 3B **40**
King's Thorn. *Here* 2C **51**
Kingstone. *Here* 2B **50**
Kingswood. *Glos* 3D **61**
Kingswood. *Here* 3D **39**
Kingswood. *Powy* 1D **31**
Kingswood. *S Glo* 2D **67**
Kington. *Here* 3A **40**
Kington. *S Glo* 3D **61**
Kinlet. *Shrp* 3D **33**
Kinmel Bay. *Cnwy* 2A **8**
Kinnerley. *Shrp* 2A **26**
Kinnersley. *Here* 1A **50**
Kinnerton. *Powy* 2D **39**
Kinnerton. *Shrp* 2A **32**
Kinsey Heath. *Ches* 3D **19**
Kinsham. *Here* 2A **40**
Kinton. *Here* 1B **40**
Kinton. *Shrp* 3A **26**
Kirkby. *Mers* 1B **10**
Kirkby Industrial Estate. *Mers* . . .1B **10**
Kirkdale. *Mers* 1A **10**
Kittle. *Swan* 1A **62**
Kivernoll. *Here* 2B **50**
Knapton Green. *Here* 3B **40**
Knelston. *Swan* 3D **55**
Knightcott. *N Som* 3A **66**
Knighton. *Powy* 1D **39**
Knighton. *Staf* 2D **27**
Knighton Common. *Worc* 1D **41**
Knightwick. *Worc* 3D **41**
Knill. *Here* 2D **39**
Knockin. *Shrp* 2A **26**
Knollbury. *Mon* 1B **66**
Knolton. *Wrex* 1A **26**
Knotty Ash. *Mers* 1B **10**
Knowbury. *Shrp* 1C **41**
Knowle. *Bris* 2D **67**

Knowle. *Shrp* 1C **41**
Knowsley. *Mers* 1B **10**
Knucklas. *Powy* 1D **39**
Knutsford. *Ches* 3D **11**
Kymin. *Mon* 1C **61**
Kynaston. *Here* 2D **51**
Kynaston. *Shrp* 2A **26**
Kynnersley. *Telf* 3D **27**
Kyre Green. *Worc* 2D **41**
Kyre Park. *Worc* 2D **41**
Kyrewood. *Worc* 2D **41**

L

Lach Dennis. *Ches* 3D **11**
Lache. *Ches* 1A **18**
Laleston. *B'end* 1D **63**
Lambston. *Pemb* 1C **53**
Lampeter. *Cdgn* 1A **46**
Lampeter Velfrey. *Pemb* 1A **54**
Lamphey. *Pemb* 2D **53**
Land Gate. *G Man* 1C **11**
Landimore. *Swan* 3D **55**
Landore. *Swan* 3B **56**
Landshipping. *Pemb* 1D **53**
Lane Head. *G Man* 1B **11**
Langland. *Swan* 1B **62**
Langridge. *Bath* 3D **67**
Lansdown. *Bath* 3D **67**
Larden Green. *Ches* 2C **19**
Larport. *Here* 2C **51**
Latteridge. *S Glo* 1D **67**
Laugharne. *Carm* 1C **55**
Lavister. *Wrex* 2A **18**
Lawrenny. *Pemb* 2D **53**
Lawton. *Here* 3B **40**
Laysters Pole. *Here* 2C **41**
Lea. *Here* 3D **51**
Lea. *Shrp* 3A **32**
  (nr. Bishop's Castle)
Lea. *Shrp* 1B **32**
  (nr. Shrewsbury)
Leachpool. *Pemb* 1C **53**
Leasowe. *Mers* 1D **9**
Leaton. *Shrp* 3B **26**
Leckwith. *V Glam* 2C **65**
Ledbury. *Here* 2D **51**
Ledgemoor. *Here* 3B **40**
Ledicot. *Here* 2B **40**
Ledsham. *Ches* 3A **10**
Lee. *Shrp* 1B **26**
Leebotwood. *Shrp* 2B **32**
Lee Brockhurst. *Shrp* 2C **27**
Leechpool. *Mon* 1C **67**
Leegomery. *Telf* 3D **27**
Leeswood. *Flin* 2D **17**
Leftwich. *Ches* 3D **11**
Leigh. *G Man* 1D **11**
Leigh. *Shrp* 1A **32**
Leighton. *Powy* 1D **31**
Leighton. *Shrp* 1D **33**
Leinthall Earls. *Here* 2B **40**
Leinthall Starkes. *Here* 2B **40**
Leintwardine. *Here* 1B **40**
Lem Hill. *Worc* 1D **41**
Leominster. *Here* 3B **40**
Letterston. *Pemb* 3C **43**
Letton. *Here* 1A **50**
  (nr. Kington)
Letton. *Here* 1A **40**
  (nr. Leintwardine)
Leweston. *Pemb* 3C **43**
Lewistown. *B'end* 1A **64**
Libanus. *Powy* 3A **48**
Lightwood Green. *Ches* 3D **19**
Lightwood Green. *Wrex* 3A **18**
Lilleshall. *Telf* 3D **27**
Lilyhurst. *Shrp* 3D **27**
Lindridge. *Worc* 2D **41**
Lingen. *Here* 2A **40**
Lingoed. *Mon* 1A **60**
Linley. *Shrp* 2A **32**
  (nr. Bishop's Castle)
Linley. *Shrp* 2D **33**
  (nr. Bridgnorth)
Linley Green. *Here* 3D **41**
Linton. *Here* 3D **51**
Linton Hill. *Here* 3D **51**
Lipley. *Shrp* 1D **27**
Liscard. *Mers* 1A **10**
Lisvane. *Card* 1C **65**
Liswerry. *Newp* 1A **66**
Litchard. *B'end* 1A **64**
Litherland. *Mers* 1A **10**
Little Barrow. *Ches* 1B **18**
Little Birch. *Here* 2C **51**
Little Bolas. *Shrp* 2D **27**
Little Bollington. *Ches* 2D **11**

Little Brampton. *Shrp* 3A **32**
Little Budworth. *Ches* 1C **19**
Little Cowarne. *Here* 3D **41**
Little Crosby. *Mers* 1A **10**
Little Dawley. *Telf* 1D **33**
Littledean. *Glos* 1D **61**
Little Dewchurch. *Here* 2C **51**
Little Drayton. *Shrp* 1D **27**
Little Garway. *Here* 3B **50**
Little Green. *Wrex* 3B **18**
Little Haven. *Pemb* 1B **52**
Little Hereford. *Here* 2C **41**
Little Hulton. *G Man* 1D **11**
Little Leigh. *Ches* 3D **11**
Little London. *Powy* 3B **30**
Little Marcle. *Here* 2D **51**
Little Mill. *Mon* 2A **60**
Little Mountain. *Flin* 1D **17**
Little Ness. *Shrp* 3B **26**
Little Neston. *Ches* 3A **10**
Little Newcastle. *Pemb* 3C **43**
Little Reynoldston. *Swan* 3D **55**
Little Ryton. *Shrp* 1B **32**
Little Soudley. *Shrp* 2D **27**
Little Stanney. *Ches* 3B **10**
Little Stretton. *Shrp* 2B **32**
Little Sutton. *Ches* 3A **10**
Littleton. *Ches* 1B **18**
Littleton-upon-Severn. *S Glo* 3C **61**
Little Wenlock. *Telf* 1D **33**
Liverpool. *Mers* 1A **10**
Liverpool Airport. *Mers* 2B **10**
Lixwm. *Flin* 3C **9**
Llaingoch. *IOA* 2B **4**
Llaithddu. *Powy* 3B **30**
Llampha. *V Glam* 2A **64**
Llan. *Powy* 1D **29**
Llanaber. *Gwyn* 3B **22**
Llanaelhaearn. *Gwyn* 3C **13**
Llanaeron. *Cdgn* 3D **35**
Llanafan. *Cdgn* 1B **36**
Llanafan-fawr. *Powy* 3A **38**
Llanafan-fechan. *Powy* 3A **38**
Llanallgo. *IOA* 2D **5**
Llanandras. *Powy* 2D **39**
Llananno. *Powy* 1B **38**
Llanarmon. *Gwyn* 1D **21**
Llanarmon Dyffryn Ceiriog. *Wrex* .1C **25**
Llanarmon-yn-Ial. *Den* 2C **17**
Llanarth. *Cdgn* 3D **35**
Llanarth. *Mon* 1A **60**
Llanarthney. *Carm* 3A **46**
Llanasa. *Flin* 2C **9**
Llanbabo. *IOA* 2C **5**
Llanbadarn Fawr. *Cdgn* 3B **28**
Llanbadarn Fynydd. *Powy* 1B **38**
Llanbadarn-y-garreg. *Powy* 1C **49**
Llanbadoc. *Mon* 2A **60**
Llanbadrig. *IOA* 1C **5**
Llanbeder. *Newp* 3A **60**
Llanbedr. *Gwyn* 2A **22**
Llanbedr. *Powy* 3D **49**
  (nr. Crickhowell)
Llanbedr. *Powy* 1C **49**
  (nr. Hay-on-Wye)
Llanbedr-Dyffryn-Clwyd. *Den* 2C **17**
Llanbedrgoch. *IOA* 2A **6**
Llanbedrog. *Gwyn* 1C **21**
Llanbedr Pont Steffan. *Cdgn* 1A **46**
Llanbedr-y-cennin. *Cnwy* 1C **15**
Llanberis. *Gwyn* 1A **14**
Llanbethery. *V Glam* 3B **64**
Llanbister. *Powy* 1C **39**
Llanblethian. *V Glam* 2B **64**
Llanboidy. *Carm* 3B **44**
Llanbradach. *Cphy* 3C **59**
Llanbrynmair. *Powy* 1D **29**
Llanbydderi. *V Glam* 3B **64**
Llancadle. *V Glam* 3B **64**
Llancarfan. *V Glam* 2B **64**
Llancatal. *V Glam* 3B **64**
Llancayo. *Mon* 2A **60**
Llancloudy. *Here* 3B **50**
Llancoch. *Powy* 1D **39**
Llancynfelyn. *Cdgn* 2B **28**
Llandaff. *Card* 2C **65**
Llandanwg. *Gwyn* 2A **22**
Llandarcy. *Neat* 3C **57**
Llandawke. *Carm* 1B **54**
Llanddaniel-Fab. *IOA* 3D **5**
Llanddarog. *Carm* 1A **56**
Llanddeiniol. *Cdgn* 1A **36**
Llanddeiniolen. *Gwyn* 1A **14**
Llandderfel. *Gwyn* 1A **24**
Llanddeusant. *Carm* 3C **47**
Llanddeusant. *IOA* 2C **5**
Llanddew. *Powy* 2B **48**
Llanddewi. *Swan* 3D **55**
Llanddewi Brefi. *Cdgn* 3B **36**

Llanddewi'r Cwm. *Powy* 1B **48**
Llanddewi Rhydderch. *Mon* 1A **60**
Llanddewi Velfrey. *Pemb* 1A **54**
Llanddewi Ystradenni. *Powy* 2C **39**
Llanddoged. *Cnwy* 1D **15**
Llanddona. *IOA* 3A **6**
Llanddowror. *Carm* 1B **54**
Llanddulas. *Cnwy* 3A **8**
Llanddwywe. *Gwyn* 2A **22**
Llanddyfnan. *IOA* 3A **6**
Llandecwyn. *Gwyn* 1B **22**
Llandefaelog Fach. *Powy* 2B **48**
Llandefaelog-tre'r-graig. *Powy* . . .2C **49**
Llandefalle. *Powy* 2C **49**
Llandegai. *Gwyn* 3A **6**
Llandegfan. *IOA* 3A **6**
Llandegla. *Den* 2C **17**
Llandegley. *Powy* 2C **39**
Llandegveth. *Mon* 3A **60**
Llandeilo. *Carm* 3B **46**
Llandeilo Graban. *Powy* 1B **48**
Llandeilo'r Fan. *Powy* 2D **47**
Llandeloy. *Pemb* 3B **42**
Llandenny. *Mon* 2B **60**
Llandevaud. *Newp* 3B **60**
Llandevenny. *Newp* 1B **66**
Llandilo. *Pemb* 3A **44**
Llandinabo. *Here* 3C **51**
Llandinam. *Powy* 3B **30**
Llandissilio. *Pemb* 3A **44**
Llandogo. *Mon* 2C **61**
Llandough. *V Glam* 2A **64**
  (nr. Cowbridge)
Llandough. *V Glam* 2C **65**
  (nr. Penarth)
Llandovery. *Carm* 2C **47**
Llandow. *V Glam* 2A **64**
Llandre. *Cdgn* 3B **28**
Llandrillo. *Den* 1B **24**
Llandrillo-yn-Rhos. *Cnwy* 2D **7**
Llandrindod. *Powy* 2B **38**
Llandrindod Wells. *Powy* 2B **38**
Llandrinio. *Powy* 3D **25**
Llandsadwrn. *Carm* 2B **46**
Llandudno. *Cnwy* 2C **7**
Llandudno Junction. *Cnwy* 3C **7**
Llandudoch. *Pemb* 1A **44**
Llandw. *V Glam* 2A **64**
Llandwrog. *Gwyn* 2D **13**
Llandybie. *Carm* 1B **56**
Llandyfaelog. *Carm* 1D **55**
Llandyfan. *Carm* 1B **56**
Llandyfriog. *Cdgn* 1C **45**
Llandyfrydog. *IOA* 2D **5**
Llandygwydd. *Cdgn* 1B **44**
Llandynan. *Den* 3C **17**
Llandyrnog. *Den* 1C **17**
Llandysilio. *Powy* 3D **25**
Llandysul. *Cdgn* 1D **45**
Llanedeyrn. *Card* 1D **65**
Llaneglwys. *Powy* 2B **48**
Llanegryn. *Gwyn* 1B **28**
Llanegwad. *Carm* 3A **46**
Llaneilian. *IOA* 1D **5**
Llanelian-yn-Rhos. *Cnwy* 3D **7**
Llanelidan. *Den* 2C **17**
Llanelieu. *Powy* 2C **49**
Llanellen. *Mon* 1A **60**
Llanelli. *Carm* 3A **56**
Llanelltyd. *Gwyn* 3C **23**
Llanelly. *Mon* 1D **59**
Llanelly Hill. *Mon* 1D **59**
Llanelwedd. *Powy* 3B **38**
Llanelwy. *Den* 3B **8**
Llanenddwyn. *Gwyn* 2A **22**
Llanengan. *Gwyn* 2B **20**
Llanerch. *Powy* 2A **32**
Llanerchymedd. *IOA* 2D **5**
Llanerfyl. *Powy* 1B **30**
Llaneuddog. *IOA* 2D **5**
Llanfachraeth. *IOA* 2C **5**
Llanfaelog. *IOA* 3C **5**
Llanfaelrhys. *Gwyn* 2B **20**
Llanfaenor. *Mon* 1B **60**
Llanfaes. *IOA* 3B **6**
Llanfaes. *Powy* 3B **48**
Llanfaethlu. *IOA* 2C **5**
Llanfaglan. *Gwyn* 1D **13**
Llanfair. *Gwyn* 2A **22**
Llanfair. *Here* 1D **49**
Llanfair Caereinion. *Powy* 1C **31**
Llanfair Clydogau. *Cdgn* 3B **36**
Llanfair Dyffryn Clwyd. *Den* 2C **17**
Llanfairfechan. *Cnwy* 3B **6**
Llanfair-Nant-Gwyn. *Pemb* 2A **44**
Llanfair Pwllgwyngyll. *IOA* 3A **6**
Llanfair Talhaiarn. *Cnwy* 3A **8**
Llanfair Waterdine. *Shrp* 1D **39**

Llanfair-ym-Muallt. *Powy* 3B **38**
Llanfairyneubwll. *IOA* 3C **5**
Llanfairynghornwy. *IOA* 1C **5**
Llanfallteg. *Carm* 1A **54**
Llanfallteg West. *Carm* 1A **54**
Llanfaredd. *Powy* 3B **38**
Llanfarian. *Cdgn* 1A **36**
Llanfechain. *Powy* 2C **25**
Llanfechell. *IOA* 1C **5**
Llanfechreth. *Gwyn* 2C **23**
Llanfendigaid. *Gwyn* 1A **28**
Llanferres. *Den* 1C **17**
Llan Ffestiniog. *Gwyn* 3C **15**
Llanfflewyn. *IOA* 2C **5**
Llanfihangel Glyn Myfyr. *Cnwy* . . .3A **16**
Llanfihangel Nant Bran. *Powy* 2A **48**
Llanfihangel-Nant-Melan. *Powy* . . .3C **39**
Llanfihangel Rhydithon. *Powy* 2C **39**
Llanfihangel Rogiet. *Mon* 1B **66**
Llanfihangel Tal-y-llyn. *Powy* 3C **49**
Llanfihangel-uwch-Gwili. *Carm* . . .3D **45**
Llanfihangel-yng-ngwynfa. *Powy* . .3B **24**
Llanfihangel yn Nhowyn. *IOA* 3C **5**
Llanfihangel-y-pennant. *Gwyn* 3A **14**
(nr. Golan)
Llanfihangel-y-pennant. *Gwyn* 1B **28**
(nr. Tywyn)
Llanfilo. *Powy* 2C **49**
Llanfinhangel-ar-Arth. *Carm* 2D **45**
Llanfinhangel-y-Creuddyn. *Cdgn* . .1B **36**
Llanfinhangel-y-traethau. *Gwyn* . . .1A **22**
Llanfleiddan. *V Glam* 2B **64**
Llanfoist. *Mon* 1D **59**
Llanfor. *Gwyn* 1A **24**
Llanfrechfa. *Torf* 3A **60**
Llanfrothen. *Gwyn* 3B **14**
Llanfrynach. *Powy* 3B **48**
Llanfwrog. *Den* 2C **17**
Llanfwrog. *IOA* 2C **5**
Llanfyllin. *Powy* 3C **25**
Llanfynydd. *Carm* 3A **46**
Llanfynydd. *Flin* 2D **17**
Llanfyrnach. *Pemb* 2B **44**
Llangadfan. *Powy* 3B **24**
Llangadog. *Carm* 3C **47**
(nr. Llandovery)
Llangadog. *Carm* 2D **55**
(nr. Llanelli)
Llangadwaladr. *IOA* 1C **13**
Llangadwaladr. *Powy* 1C **25**
Llangaffo. *IOA* 1D **13**
Llangain. *Carm* 1C **55**
Llangammarch Wells. *Powy* 1A **48**
Llangan. *V Glam* 2A **64**
Llangarron. *Here* 3C **51**
Llangasty-Talyllyn. *Powy* 3C **49**
Llangathen. *Carm* 3A **46**
Llangattock. *Powy* 1D **59**
Llangattock Lingoed. *Mon* 3A **50**
Llangattock-Vibon-Avel. *Mon* 1B **60**
Llangedwyn. *Powy* 2C **25**
Llangefni. *IOA* 3D **5**
Llangeinor. *B'end* 1A **64**
Llangeitho. *Cdgn* 3B **36**
Llangeler. *Carm* 2C **45**
Llangelynin. *Gwyn* 1A **28**
Llangendeirne. *Carm* 1D **55**
Llangennech. *Carm* 2A **56**
Llangennith. *Swan* 3D **55**
Llangenny. *Powy* 1D **59**
Llangernyw. *Cnwy* 1D **15**
Llangian. *Gwyn* 2B **20**
Llangiwg. *Neat* 2C **57**
Llangloffan. *Pemb* 2C **43**
Llanglydwen. *Carm* 3A **44**
Llangoed. *IOA* 3B **6**
Llangoedmor. *Cdgn* 1B **44**
Llangollen. *Den* 3D **17**
Llangolman. *Pemb* 3A **44**
Llangorse. *Powy* 3C **49**
Llangorwen. *Cdgn* 3B **28**
Llangovan. *Mon* 2B **60**
Llangower. *Gwyn* 1A **24**
Llangranog. *Cdgn* 3C **35**
Llangristiolus. *IOA* 3D **5**
Llangrove. *Here* 1C **61**
Llangua. *Mon* 3A **50**
Llangunllo. *Powy* 1D **39**
Llangunnor. *Carm* 3D **45**
Llangurig. *Powy* 1A **38**
Llangwm. *Cnwy* 3A **16**
Llangwm. *Mon* 2B **60**
Llangwm. *Pemb* 2C **53**
Llangwm-isaf. *Mon* 2B **60**
Llangwnnadl. *Gwyn* 1B **20**
Llangwyfan. *Den* 1C **17**
Llangwyfan-isaf. *IOA* 1C **13**
Llangwyllog. *IOA* 3D **5**
Llangwyryfon. *Cdgn* 1A **36**

Llangybi. *Cdgn* 3B **36**
Llangybi. *Gwyn* 3D **13**
Llangybi. *Mon* 3A **60**
Llangyfelach. *Swan* 3B **56**
Llangynhafal. *Den* 1C **17**
Llangynidr. *Powy* 1C **59**
Llangynin. *Carm* 1B **54**
Llangynog. *Carm* 1C **55**
Llangynog. *Powy* 2B **24**
Llangynwyd. *B'end* 1D **63**
Llanhamlach. *Powy* 3B **48**
Llanharan. *Rhon* 1B **64**
Llanharry. *Rhon* 1B **64**
Llanhennock. *Mon* 3A **60**
Llanhilleth. *Blae* 2D **59**
Llanidloes. *Powy* 1A **38**
Llaniestyn. *Gwyn* 1B **20**
Llanigon. *Powy* 1D **49**
Llanilar. *Cdgn* 1B **36**
Llanilid. *Rhon* 1A **64**
Llanilltud Fawr. *V Glam* 3C **63**
Llanishen. *Card* 1C **65**
Llanishen. *Mon* 2B **60**
Llanllawddog. *Carm* 3D **45**
Llanllechid. *Gwyn* 1B **14**
Llanllowell. *Mon* 3A **60**
Llanllugan. *Powy* 1B **30**
Llanllwch. *Carm* 1C **55**
Llanllwchaiarn. *Powy* 2C **31**
Llanllwni. *Carm* 2D **45**
Llanllyfni. *Gwyn* 2D **13**
Llanmadoc. *Swan* 3D **55**
Llanmaes. *V Glam* 3A **64**
Llanmartin. *Newp* 1A **66**
Llanmerewig. *Powy* 2C **31**
Llanmihangel. *V Glam* 2A **64**
Llan-mill. *Pemb* 1A **54**
Llanmiloe. *Carm* 3A **54**
Llanmorlais. *Swan* 3A **56**
Llannefydd. *Cnwy* 3A **8**
Llannon. *Carm* 2A **56**
Llan-non. *Cdgn* 2A **36**
Llannor. *Gwyn* 1C **21**
Llanpumsaint. *Carm* 3D **45**
Llanrhaeadr. *Den* 1B **16**
Llanrhaeadr-ym-Mochnant.
Powy 2C **25**
Llanrhidian. *Swan* 3D **55**
Llanrhos. *Cnwy* 2C **7**
Llanrhyddlad. *IOA* 2C **5**
Llanrhystud. *Cdgn* 2A **36**
Llanrian. *Pemb* 2B **42**
Llanrothal. *Here* 1B **60**
Llanrug. *Gwyn* 1A **14**
Llanrumney. *Card* 1D **65**
Llanrwst. *Cnwy* 1C **15**
Llansadurnen. *Carm* 1B **54**
Llansadwrn. *IOA* 3A **6**
Llansaint. *Carm* 2C **55**
Llansamlet. *Swan* 3B **56**
Llansanffraid Glan Conwy. *Cnwy* . .3D **7**
Llansannan. *Cnwy* 1A **16**
Llansannor. *V Glam* 2A **64**
Llansantffraed. *Cdgn* 2D **35**
Llansantffraed. *Powy* 3C **49**
Llansantffraed Cwmdeuddwr.
Powy 2A **38**
Llansantffraed in Elwel. *Powy* 3B **38**
Llansantffraid-ym-Mechain.
Powy 2D **25**
Llansawel. *Carm* 2B **46**
Llansawel. *Neat* 3B **56**
Llansilin. *Powy* 2D **25**
Llansoy. *Mon* 2B **60**
Llanspyddid. *Powy* 3B **48**
Llanstadwell. *Pemb* 2C **53**
Llansteffan. *Carm* 1C **55**
Llanstephan. *Powy* 1C **49**
Llanteg. *Pemb* 1A **54**
Llanthony. *Mon* 3D **49**
Llantilio Crossenny. *Mon* 1A **60**
Llantilio Pertholey. *Mon* 1A **60**
Llantood. *Pemb* 1A **44**
Llantrisant. *Mon* 3A **60**
Llantrisant. *Rhon* 1B **64**
Llantrithyd. *V Glam* 2B **64**
Llantwit Fardre. *Rhon* 1B **64**
Llantwit Major. *V Glam* 3A **64**
Llanuwchllyn. *Gwyn* 1D **23**
Llanvaches. *Newp* 3B **60**
Llanvair Discoed. *Mon* 3B **60**
Llanvapley. *Mon* 1A **60**
Llanvetherine. *Mon* 1A **60**
Llanveynoe. *Here* 2A **50**
Llanvihangel Crucorney. *Mon* 3A **50**
Llanvihangel Gobion. *Mon* 2A **60**
Llanvihangel Ystern-Llewern.
Mon 1B **60**

Llanwarne. *Here* 3C **51**
Llanwddyn. *Powy* 3B **24**
Llanwenarth. *Mon* 1D **59**
Llanwenog. *Cdgn* 1D **45**
Llanwern. *Newp* 1A **66**
Llanwinio. *Carm* 3B **44**
Llanwnda. *Gwyn* 2D **13**
Llanwnda. *Pemb* 2C **43**
Llanwnnen. *Cdgn* 1A **46**
Llanwnog. *Powy* 2B **30**
Llanwrda. *Carm* 2C **47**
Llanwrin. *Powy* 1A **30**
Llanwrthwl. *Powy* 2A **38**
Llanwrtud. *Powy* 1D **47**
Llanwrtyd. *Powy* 1D **47**
Llanwrtyd Wells. *Powy* 1D **47**
Llanwyddelan. *Powy* 1B **30**
Llanyblodwel. *Shrp* 2D **25**
Llanybri. *Carm* 1C **55**
Llanybydder. *Carm* 1A **46**
Llanycefn. *Pemb* 3D **43**
Llanychaer. *Pemb* 2C **43**
Llanycil. *Gwyn* 1A **24**
Llanymawddwy. *Gwyn* 3A **24**
Llanymddyfri. *Carm* 2C **47**
Llanymynech. *Powy* 2D **25**
Llanynghenedl. *IOA* 2C **5**
Llanynys. *Den* 1C **17**
Llan-y-pwll. *Wrex* 2A **18**
Llanyrafon. *Torf* 3A **60**
Llanyre. *Powy* 2B **38**
Llanystumdwy. *Gwyn* 1D **21**
Llanywern. *Powy* 3C **49**
Llawhaden. *Pemb* 1D **53**
Llawndy. *Flin* 2C **9**
Llawnt. *Shrp* 1D **25**
Llawr Dref. *Gwyn* 2B **20**
Llawryglyn. *Powy* 1A **30**
Llay. *Wrex* .2A **18**
Llechfaen. *Powy* 3B **48**
Llechryd. *Cphy* 1A **58**
Llechryd. *Cdgn* 1B **44**
Llechrydau. *Wrex* 1D **25**
Lledrod. *Cdgn* 1B **36**
Llethrid. *Swan* 3A **56**
Llidiad-Nenog. *Carm* 2A **46**
Llidiardau. *Gwyn* 1D **23**
Llidiart y Parc. *Den* 3C **17**
Llithfaen. *Gwyn* 3C **13**
Lloc. *Flin* 3C **9**
Llong. *Flin* .1D **17**
Llowes. *Powy* 1C **49**
Lloyney. *Powy* 1D **39**
Llundain-fach. *Cdgn* 3A **36**
Llwydcoed. *Rhon* 2A **58**
Llwyncelyn. *Cdgn* 3D **35**
Llwyncelyn. *Swan* 2B **56**
Llwyndaffydd. *Cdgn* 3C **35**
Llwynderw. *Powy* 1D **31**
Llwyn-du. *Mon* 1D **59**
Llwyngwril. *Gwyn* 1A **28**
Llwynhendy. *Carm* 3A **56**
Llwynmawr. *Wrex* 1D **25**
Llwyn-on Village. *Mer T* 1B **58**
Llwyn-teg. *Carm* 2A **56**
Llwyn-y-brain. *Carm* 1A **54**
Llwynygog. *Powy* 2D **29**
Llwyn-y-groes. *Cdgn* 3A **36**
Llwynypia. *Rhon* 3A **58**
Llynclys. *Shrp* 2D **25**
Llynfaes. *IOA* 3D **5**
Llysfaen. *Cnwy* 3D **7**
Llyswen. *Powy* 2C **49**
Llysworney. *V Glam* 2A **64**
Llys-y-fran. *Pemb* 3D **43**
Llywel. *Powy* 2D **47**
Llywernog. *Cdgn* 3C **29**
Locking. *N Som* 3A **66**
Lockleywood. *Shrp* 2D **27**
Logaston. *Here* 3A **40**
Loggerheads. *Staf* 1D **27**
Login. *Carm* 3A **44**
Long Ashton. *N Som* 2C **67**
Longden. *Shrp* 1B **32**
Longden Common. *Shrp* 1B **32**
Longdon on Tern. *Telf* 3D **27**
Longford. *Shrp* 1D **27**
Longford. *Telf* 3D **27**
Long Green. *Ches* 3B **10**
Longhope. *Glos* 1D **61**
Long Lane. *Telf* 3D **27**
Longley Green. *Worc* 3D **41**
Long Meadowend. *Shrp* 3B **32**
Longnor. *Shrp* 1B **32**
Longshaw. *G Man* 1C **11**
Longslow. *Shrp* 1D **27**
Longtown. *Here* 3A **50**
Longville in the Dale. *Shrp* 2C **33**
Loppington. *Shrp* 2B **26**

Lostock Gralam. *Ches* 3D **11**
Lostock Green. *Ches* 3D **11**
Loughor. *Swan* 3A **56**
Loughton. *Shrp* 3D **33**
Loveston. *Pemb* 2D **53**
Lowe. *Shrp* 1C **27**
Lower Brynamman. *Neat* 1C **57**
Lower Bullingham. *Here* 2C **51**
Lower Cam. *Glos* 2D **61**
Lower Chapel. *Powy* 2B **48**
Lower Down. *Shrp* 3A **32**
Lower Egleton. *Here* 1D **51**
Lower Failand. *N Som* 2C **67**
Lower Faintree. *Shrp* 3D **33**
Lower Frankton. *Shrp* 1A **26**
Lower Hardwick. *Here* 3B **40**
Lower Hayton. *Shrp* 3C **33**
Lower Hergest. *Here* 3D **39**
Lower Hordley. *Shrp* 2A **26**
Lower Kinnerton. *Ches* 1A **18**
Lower Langford. *N Som* 3B **66**
Lower Ledwyche. *Shrp* 1C **41**
Lower Ley. *Glos* 1D **61**
Lower Llanfadog. *Powy* 2A **38**
Lower Lydbrook. *Glos* 1C **61**
Lower Lye. *Here* 2B **40**
Lower Machen. *Newp* 1D **65**
Lower Maes-coed. *Here* 2A **50**
Lower Meend. *Glos* 2C **61**
Lower Morton. *S Glo* 3D **61**
Lower Mountain. *Flin* 2A **18**
Lower Penarth. *V Glam* 3C **65**
Lower Peover. *Ches* 3D **11**
Lower Sketty. *Swan* 3B **56**
Lower Soudley. *Glos* 1D **61**
Lower Town. *Here* 1D **51**
Lower Town. *Pemb* 2C **43**
Lower Walton. *Warr* 2D **11**
Lower Welson. *Here* 3D **39**
Lower Whitley. *Ches* 3D **11**
Lower Wych. *Ches* 3B **18**
Lowton. *G Man* 1D **11**
Lowton Common. *G Man* 1D **11**
Lucton. *Here* 2B **40**
Ludchurch. *Pemb* 1A **54**
Ludford. *Shrp* 1C **41**
Ludlow. *Shrp* 1C **41**
Lugg Green. *Here* 2B **40**
Lugwardine. *Here* 1C **51**
Lulham. *Here* 1B **50**
Lulsgate Bottom. *N Som* 3C **67**
Lulsley. *Worc* 3D **41**
Lunnon. *Swan* 1A **62**
Lunt. *Mers* .1A **10**
Luston. *Here* 2B **40**
Luxley. *Glos* 3D **51**
Lydbury North. *Shrp* 3A **32**
Lydham. *Shrp* 2A **32**
Lydney. *Glos* 2D **61**
Lydstep. *Pemb* 3D **53**
Lye, The. *Shrp* 2D **33**
Lymm. *Warr* 2D **11**
Lyneal. *Shrp* 1B **26**
Lyne Down. *Here* 2D **51**
Lyonshall. *Here* 3A **40**

M

Machen. *Cphy* 1D **65**
Machroes. *Gwyn* 2C **21**
Machynlleth. *Powy* 1C **29**
Madeley. *Telf* 1D **33**
Madley. *Here* 2B **50**
Maenaddwyn. *IOA* 2D **5**
Maenclochog. *Pemb* 3D **43**
Maendy. *V Glam* 2B **64**
Maentwrog. *Gwyn* 3B **14**
Maen-y-groes. *Cdgn* 1A **44**
Maerdy. *Carm* 3B **46**
Maerdy. *Cnwy* 3B **16**
Maerdy. *Rhon* 3A **58**
Maesbrook. *Shrp* 2A **26**
Maesbury. *Shrp* 2A **26**
Maesbury Marsh. *Shrp* 2A **26**
Maes-glas. *Flin* 3C **9**
Maesgwyn-Isaf. *Powy* 3C **25**
Maeshafn. *Den* 1D **17**
Maes Llyn. *Cdgn* 1C **45**
Maesmynis. *Powy* 1B **48**
Maesteg. *B'end* 3D **57**
Maestir. *Cdgn* 1A **46**
Maesybont. *Carm* 1A **56**
Maesycrugiau. *Carm* 1D **45**
Maesycwmmer. *Cphy* 3C **59**
Maesyrhandir. *Powy* 2B **30**
Maghull. *Mers* 1A **10**
Magor. *Mon* 1B **66**
Magwyr. *Mon* 1B **66**

Maiden Wells. *Pemb* 3C **53**
Maindee. *Newp* 1A **66**
Mainstone. *Shrp* 3D **31**
Malinslee. *Telf* 1D **33**
Malltraeth. *IOA* 1D **13**
Mallwyd. *Gwyn* 3D **23**
Malpas. *Ches* 3B **18**
Malpas. *Newp* 3D **59**
Malswick. *Glos* 3D **51**
Mamble. *Worc* 1D **41**
Mamhilad. *Mon* 2A **60**
Manafon. *Powy* 1C **31**
Mancot. *Flin* 1A **18**
Mangotsfield. *S Glo* 2D **67**
Manley. *Ches* 3C **11**
Manmoel. *Cphy* 2C **59**
Manorbier. *Pemb* 3D **53**
Manorbier Newton. *Pemb* 3D **53**
Manorowen. *Pemb* 2C **43**
Mansell Gamage. *Here* 1A **50**
Mansell Lacy. *Here* 1B **50**
Marbury. *Ches* 3C **19**
Marchamley. *Shrp* 2C **27**
Marchwiel. *Wrex* 3A **18**
Marcross. *V Glam* 3A **64**
Marden. *Here* 1C **51**
Mardu. *Shrp* 3D **31**
Mardy. *Mon* 1A **60**
Marford. *Wrex* 2A **18**
Margam. *Neat* 1C **63**
Marian Cwm. *Den* 3B **8**
Mariandyrys. *IOA* 2B **6**
Marian-glas. *IOA* 2A **6**
Marian-y-de. *Gwyn* 1C **21**
Marion-y-mor. *Gwyn* 1C **21**
Market Drayton. *Shrp* 1D **27**
Markham. *Cphy* 2C **59**
Marksbury. *Bath* 3D **67**
Marley Green. *Ches* 3C **19**
Marloes. *Pemb* 2A **52**
Marlow. *Here* 1B **40**
Marros. *Carm* 2B **54**
Marshbrook. *Shrp* 3B **32**
Marshfield. *Newp* 1D **65**
Marsh Green. *Telf* 3D **27**
Marsh, The. *Powy* 2A **32**
Marsh, The. *Shrp* 2D **27**
Marston. *Ches* 3D **11**
Marston. *Here* 3A **40**
Marston Stannett. *Here* 3C **41**
Marstow. *Here* 1C **61**
Martinscroft. *Warr* 2D **11**
Martletwy. *Pemb* 1D **53**
Marton. *Shrp* 2B **26**
(nr. Myddle)
Marton. *Shrp* 1D **31**
(nr. Worthen)
Mathern. *Mon* 3C **61**
Mathon. *Here* 1D **51**
Mathry. *Pemb* 2B **42**
Maund Bryan. *Here* 3C **41**
Mawdlam. *B'end* 1D **63**
Maw Green. *Ches* 2D **19**
Mayals. *Swan* 1B **62**
Mayhill. *Swan* 3B **56**
Maypole. *Mon* 1B **60**
Mayshill. *S Glo* 1D **67**
Meadgate. *Bath* 3D **67**
Meadowbank. *Ches* 1D **19**
Meadow Green. *Here* 3D **41**
Meadowtown. *Shrp* 1A **32**
Medlicott. *Shrp* 2B **32**
Meeson. *Telf* 2D **27**
Meidrim. *Carm* 3B **44**
Meifod. *Powy* 3C **25**
Meinciau. *Carm* 1D **55**
Meliden. *Den* 2B **8**
Melinbyrhedyn. *Powy* 2D **29**
Melincourt. *Neat* 2D **57**
Melin-y-coed. *Cnwy* 1D **15**
Melin-y-ddol. *Powy* 1B **30**
Melin-y-wig. *Den* 3B **16**
Melling. *Mers* 1A **10**
Melling Mount. *Mers* 1B **10**
Melverley. *Shrp* 3A **26**
Melverley Green. *Shrp* 3A **26**
Menai Bridge. *IOA* 3A **6**
Menithwood. *Worc* 2D **41**
Meole Brace. *Shrp* 3B **26**
Meols. *Mers* 2D **9**
Merbach. *Here* 1A **50**
Mere. *Ches* 2D **11**
Mere Heath. *Ches* 3D **11**
Meretown. *Staf* 2D **27**
Merlin's Bridge. *Pemb* 1C **53**
Merrington. *Shrp* 2B **26**
Merrion. *Pemb* 3C **53**
Merthyr. *Carm* 3C **45**
Merthyr Cynog. *Powy* 2A **48**

Merthyr Dyfan. *V Glam* 3C **65**
Merthyr Mawr. *B'end* 2D **63**
Merthyr Tudful. *Mer T* 2B **58**
Merthyr Tydfil. *Mer T* 2B **58**
Merthyr Vale. *Mer T* 2B **58**
Michaelchurch. *Here* 3C **51**
Michaelchurch Escley. *Here* 2A **50**
Michaelchurch-on-Arrow. *Powy* . . .3D **39**
Michaelston-le-Pit. *V Glam* 2C **65**
Michaelston-y-Vedw. *Newp* 1D **65**
Mickle Trafford. *Ches* 1B **18**
Middlehope. *Shrp* 3B **32**
Middle Maes-coed. *Here* 2A **50**
Middleton. *Here* 2C **41**
Middleton. *Shrp* 1C **41**
(nr. Ludlow)
Middleton. *Shrp* 2A **26**
(nr. Oswestry)
Middleton. *Swan* 3D **55**
Middleton on the Hill. *Here* 2C **41**
Middleton Priors. *Shrp* 2D **33**
Middleton Scriven. *Shrp* 3D **33**
Middletown. *Powy* 3A **26**
Middlewich. *Ches* 1D **19**
Milbury Heath. *S Glo* 3D **61**
Milebrook. *Powy* 1A **40**
Miles Hope. *Here* 2C **41**
Milford. *Powy* 2B **30**
Milford Haven. *Pemb* 2C **53**
Milkwall. *Glos* 2C **61**
Millend. *Glos* 3D **61**
Mill Green. *Shrp* 2D **27**
Millhalf. *Here* 1D **49**
Milson. *Shrp* 1D **41**
Milton. *N Som* 3A **66**
Milton. *Pemb* 2D **53**
Milton Green. *Ches* 2B **18**
Minera. *Wrex* 2D **17**
Minffordd. *Gwyn* 1A **22**
Minllyn. *Gwyn* 3D **23**
Minsterley. *Shrp* 1A **32**
Minton. *Shrp* 2B **32**
Minwear. *Pemb* 1D **53**
Miskin. *Rhon* 1B **64**
Mitcheldean. *Glos* 1D **61**
Mitchel Troy. *Mon* 1B **60**
Mitcheltroy Common. *Mon* 2B **60**
Moccas. *Here* 1A **50**
Mochdre. *Cnwy* 3D **7**
Mochdre. *Powy* 3B **30**
Moelfre. *Cnwy* 3A **8**
Moelfre. *IOA* 2A **6**
Moelfre. *Powy* 2C **25**
Mold. *Flin* 1D **17**
Mollington. *Ches* 3A **10**
Monachty. *Cdgn* 2A **36**
Monaughty. *Powy* 2D **39**
Monington. *Pemb* 1A **44**
Monkhide. *Here* 1D **51**
Monkhopton. *Shrp* 2D **33**
Monkland. *Here* 3B **40**
Monknash. *V Glam* 2A **64**
Monkswood. *Mon* 2A **60**
Monkton. *Pemb* 2C **53**
Monmarsh. *Here* 1C **51**
Monmouth. *Mon* 1C **61**
Monnington on Wye. *Here* 1A **50**
Montford. *Shrp* 3B **26**
Montford Bridge. *Shrp* 3B **26**
Montgomery. *Powy* 2D **31**
Moorcot. *Here* 3A **40**
Moore. *Hal* 2C **11**
Moorend. *Glos* 2D **61**
Moorhampton. *Here* 1A **50**
Moortown. *Telf* 3D **27**
Morda. *Shrp* 2D **25**
Mordiford. *Here* 2C **51**
More. *Shrp* 2A **32**
Morehouse, The. *Shrp* 2C **33**
Moreton. *Here* 2C **41**
Moreton. *Mers* 1D **9**
Moreton Corbet. *Shrp* 2C **27**
Moreton Jeffries. *Here* 1D **51**
Moreton on Lugg. *Here* 1C **51**
Moreton Say. *Shrp* 1D **27**
Morfa. *Cdgn* 3C **35**
Morfa Bach. *Carm* 1C **55**
Morfa Bychan. *Gwyn* 1A **22**
Morfa Glas. *Neat* 2D **57**
Morfa Nefyn. *Gwyn* 3B **12**
Morganstown. *Card* 1C **65**
Moriah. *Cdgn* 1B **36**
Morriston. *Swan* 3B **56**
Mortimer's Cross. *Here* 2B **40**
Morton. *Shrp* 2D **25**
Morton. *S Glo* 3D **61**
Morton Mill. *Shrp* 2C **27**
Morvil. *Pemb* 2D **43**
Morville. *Shrp* 2D **33**

Mose. *Shrp* 2D **33**
Moss. *Wrex* 2A **18**
Moss Bank. *Mers* 1C **11**
Mossbrow. *G Man* 2D **11**
Mossley Hill. *Mers* 2A **10**
Moss Side. *Mers* 1A **10**
Moston. *Shrp* 2C **27**
Moston Green. *Ches* 1D **19**
Mostyn. *Flin* 2C **9**
Mouldsworth. *Ches* 3C **11**
Moulton. *Ches* 1D **19**
Moulton. *V Glam* 2B **64**
Mountain Ash. *Rhon* 3B **58**
Mountain Water. *Pemb* 3C **43**
Mounton. *Mon* 3C **61**
Moylgrove. *Pemb* 1A **44**
Much Birch. *Here* 2C **51**
Much Cowarne. *Here* 1D **51**
Much Dewchurch. *Here* 2B **50**
Much Marcle. *Here* 2D **51**
Much Wenlock. *Shrp* 1D **33**
Mucklestone. *Staf* 1D **27**
Muckleton. *Shrp* 2C **27**
Muckley. *Shrp* 2D **33**
Mumbles, The. *Swan* 1B **62**
Munderfield Row. *Here* 3D **41**
Munderfield Stocks. *Here* 3D **41**
Munsley. *Here* 1D **51**
Munslow. *Shrp* 3C **33**
Murdishaw. *Hal* 2C **11**
Murton. *Swan* 1A **62**
Muxton. *Telf* 3D **27**
Mwmbwls. *Swan* 1B **62**
Myddfai. *Carm* 2C **47**
Myddle. *Shrp* 2B **26**
Mydroilyn. *Cdgn* 3D **35**
Mynachlog-ddu. *Pemb* 2A **44**
Mynydd-bach. *Mon* 3B **60**
Mynydd Isa. *Flin* 1D **17**
Mynyddislwyn. *Cphy* 3C **59**
Mynydd Llandegai. *Gwyn* 1B **14**
Mynydd Mechell. *IOA* 1C **5**
Mynydd-y-briw. *Powy* 2C **25**
Mynyddygarreg. *Carm* 2D **55**
Mynytho. *Gwyn* 1C **21**
Mytton. *Shrp* 3B **26**

N

Nailbridge. *Glos* 1D **61**
Nailsea. *N Som* 2B **66**
Nanhyfer. *Pemb* 1D **43**
Nannerch. *Flin* 1C **17**
Nant-ddu. *Rhon* 1B **58**
Nanternis. *Cdgn* 3C **35**
Nantgaredig. *Carm* 3D **45**
Nantgarw. *Rhon* 1C **65**
Nant Glas. *Powy* 2A **38**
Nantglyn. *Den* 1B **16**
Nantgwyn. *Powy* 1A **38**
Nantlle. *Gwyn* 2A **14**
Nantmawr. *Shrp* 2D **25**
Nantmel. *Powy* 2B **38**
Nantmor. *Gwyn* 3B **14**
Nant Peris. *Gwyn* 2B **14**
Nantwich. *Ches* 2D **19**
Nant-y-bai. *Carm* 1C **47**
Nant-y-bwch. *Blae* 1C **59**
Nant-y-Derry. *Mon* 2A **60**
Nant-y-dugoed. *Powy* 3A **24**
Nant-y-felin. *Cnwy* 3B **6**
Nantyffyllon. *B'end* 3D **57**
Nantyglo. *Blae* 1C **59**
Nant-y-meichiaid. *Powy* 3C **25**
Nant-y-moel. *B'end* 3A **58**
Nant-y-Pandy. *Cnwy* 3B **6**
Narberth. *Pemb* 1A **54**
Narberth Bridge. *Pemb* 1A **54**
Narth, The. *Mon* 2C **61**
Nasareth. *Gwyn* 3D **13**
Nash. *Here* 2A **40**
Nash. *Newp* 1A **66**
Nash. *Shrp* 1D **41**
Neath. *Neat* 3C **57**
Neath Abbey. *Neat* 3C **57**
Nebo. *Cdgn* 2A **36**
Nebo. *Cnwy* 2D **15**
Nebo. *Gwyn* 2D **13**
Nebo. *IOA* 1D **5**
Neen Savage. *Shrp* 1D **41**
Neen Sollars. *Shrp* 1D **41**
Neenton. *Shrp* 3D **33**
Nefyn. *Gwyn* 3C **13**
Nelly Andrews Green. *Powy* 1D **31**
Nelson. *Cphy* 3C **59**
Nempnett Thrubwell. *Bath* 3C **67**
Nercwys. *Flin* 1D **17**
Ness. *Ches* 3A **10**

Nesscliffe. *Shrp* 3A **26**
Neston. *Ches* 3D **9**
Netchwood. *Shrp* 2D **33**
Netherend. *Glos* 2C **61**
Netherton. *Here* 3C **51**
Netherton. *Mers* 1A **10**
Netley. *Shrp* 1B **32**
Neuadd. *Carm* 3C **47**
Neuadd. *Powy* 1B **30**
Nevern. *Pemb* 1D **43**
Newborough. *IOA* 1D **13**
Newbridge. *Cphy* 3D **59**
Newbridge. *Cdgn* 3A **36**
Newbridge. *Pemb* 2C **43**
Newbridge. *Wrex* 3D **17**
Newbridge-on-Usk. *Mon* 3A **60**
Newbridge on Wye. *Powy* 3B **38**
New Brighton. *Flin* 1D **17**
New Broughton. *Wrex* 2A **18**
Newcastle. *B'end* 1D **63**
Newcastle. *Mon* 1B **60**
Newcastle. *Shrp* 3D **31**
Newcastle Emlyn. *Carm* 1C **45**
Newchapel. *Pemb* 2B **44**
Newchapel. *Powy* 3A **30**
Newchurch. *Carm* 3C **45**
Newchurch. *Here* 3A **40**
Newchurch. *Mon* 3B **60**
Newchurch. *Powy* 3D **39**
New Cross. *Cdgn* 1B **36**
Newent. *Glos* 3D **51**
New Ferry. *Mers* 2A **10**
Newgate. *Pemb* 3B **42**
Newhall. *Ches* 3D **19**
New Hedges. *Pemb* 2A **54**
New Inn. *Carm* 2D **45**
New Inn. *Mon* 3A **60**
New Inn. *Torf* 3A **60**
New Invention. *Shrp* 1D **39**
Newland. *Glos* 2C **61**
Newlands Park. *IOA* 2B **4**
New Lane End. *Warr* 1D **11**
New Marton. *Shrp* 1A **26**
New Mills. *Mon* 2C **61**
New Mills. *Powy* 1B **30**
New Moat. *Pemb* 3D **43**
Newnham. *Glos* 1D **61**
Newnham Bridge. *Worc* 2D **41**
Newport. *Glos* 3D **61**
Newport. *Newp* 1A **66**
Newport. *Pemb* 2D **43**
Newport. *Telf* 3D **27**
New Quay. *Cdgn* 3C **35**
New Radnor. *Powy* 2D **39**
New Row. *Cdgn* 1C **37**
New Street. *Here* 3A **40**
Newstreet Lane. *Shrp* 1D **27**
Newton. *B'end* 2D **63**
Newton. *Ches* 3B **18**
(nr. Chester)
Newton. *Ches* 2C **19**
(nr. Tattenhall)
Newton. *Here* 2A **50**
(nr. Ewyas Harold)
Newton. *Here* 3C **41**
(nr. Leominster)
Newton. *Mers* 2D **9**
Newton. *Shrp* 2D **33**
(nr. Bridgnorth)
Newton. *Shrp* 1B **26**
(nr. Wem)
Newton. *Swan* 1B **62**
Newton Green. *Mon* 3C **61**
Newton-le-Willows. *Mers* 1C **11**
Newton on the Hill. *Shrp* 2B **26**
Newton St Loe. *Bath* 3D **67**
Newtown. *Ches* 3D **19**
Newtown. *Glos* 2D **61**
Newtown. *Here* 2D **51**
(nr. Ledbury)
Newtown. *Here* 2C **51**
(nr. Little Dewchurch)
Newtown. *Here* 1D **51**
(nr. Stretton Grandison)
Newtown. *Powy* 2C **31**
Newtown. *Rhon* 3B **58**
Newtown. *Shrp* 1B **26**
New Tredegar. *Cphy* 2C **59**
Nextend. *Here* 3A **40**
Neyland. *Pemb* 2C **53**
Nib Heath. *Shrp* 3B **26**
Nicholaston. *Swan* 1A **62**
Niwbwrch. *IOA* 1D **13**
Nobold. *Shrp* 3B **26**
Nolton. *Pemb* 1B **52**
Nolton Haven. *Pemb* 1B **52**
No Man's Heath. *Ches* 3C **19**
Noneley. *Shrp* 2B **26**

Norbridge. Here 1D 51
Norbury. Ches 3C 19
Norbury. Shrp 2A 32
Nordley. Shrp 2D 33
Norley. Ches 3C 11
Norris Green. Mers 1A 10
North Cornelly. B'end 1D 63
North End. N Som 3B 66
North Nibley. Glos 3D 61
Northop. Flin 1D 17
Northop Hall. Flin 1D 17
North Stoke. Bath 3D 67
Northway. Swan 1A 62
North Weston. N Som 2B 66
Northwich. Ches 3D 11
North Wick. Bath 3C 67
Northwick. S Glo 1C 67
North Widcombe. Bath 3C 67
Northwood. Shrp 1B 26
Northwood Green. Glos 1D 61
Norton. Hal 2C 11
Norton. Mon 3B 50
Norton. Powy 2A 40
Norton. Shrp 3B 32
 (nr. Ludlow)
Norton. Shrp 1D 33
 (nr. Madeley)
Norton. Shrp 1C 33
 (nr. Shrewsbury)
Norton. Swan 1B 62
Norton Canon. Here 1A 50
Norton Hawkfield. Bath 3C 67
Norton in Hales. Shrp 1D 27
Norton Malreward. Bath 3D 67
Nottage. B'end 2D 63
Nox. Shrp 3B 26
Noyadd Trefawr. Cdgn 1B 44
Nurston. V Glam 3B 64

O

Oakdale. Cphy 3C 59
Oakengates. Telf 3D 27
Oakenholt. Flin 3D 9
Oakford. Cdgn 3D 35
Oaklands. Powy 3B 38
Oakley Park. Powy 3A 30
Oakmere. Ches 1C 19
Oaks. Shrp 1B 32
Occlestone Green. Ches 1D 19
Ocle Pychard. Here 1C 51
Odd Down. Bath 3D 67
Ogmore. V Glam 2D 63
Ogmore-by-Sea. V Glam 2D 63
Ogmore Vale. B'end 1A 64
Oldbury. Shrp 2D 33
Oldbury-on-Severn. S Glo 3D 61
Oldcastle. Mon 3A 50
Oldcastle Heath. Ches 3B 18
Old Colwyn. Cnwy 3D 7
Old Down. S Glo 1D 67
Oldfield. Shrp 3D 33
Old Forge. Here 3D 51
Oldland. S Glo 2D 67
Old Llanberis. Gwyn 2B 14
Oldmixon. N Som 3A 66
Old Park. Telf 1D 33
Old Radnor. Powy 3D 39
Old Swan. Mers 1A 10
Oldwalls. Swan 3D 55
Oldwood Common. Worc 2C 41
Ollerton. Shrp 2D 27
Olmarch. Cdgn 3B 36
Olveston. S Glo 1D 67
Onen. Mon 1B 60
Ongar Street. Here 2A 40
Onibury. Shrp 1B 40
Onllwyn. Neat 1D 57
Onneley. Shrp 1A 28
Orcop. Here 3B 50
Orcop Hill. Here 3B 50
Oreton. Shrp 3D 33
Orford. Warr 1D 11
Orleton. Here 2B 40
Orleton. Worc 2D 41
Orleton Common. Here 2B 40
Orrell. Mers 1A 10
Osbaston. Shrp 2D 25
Oscroft. Ches 1C 19
Oswestry. Shrp 2D 25
Otterspool. Mers 2A 10
Oughtrington. Warr 2D 11
Over. Ches 1D 19
Over. S Glo 1C 67
Over Monnow. Mon 1C 61
Overpool. Ches 3A 10
Overton. Ches 3C 11

Overton. Shrp 3D 33
 (nr. Bridgnorth)
Overton. Shrp 1C 41
 (nr. Ludlow)
Overton. Swan 1A 62
Overton. Wrex 3A 18
Owlbury. Shrp 2A 32
Owrytn. Wrex 3A 18
Oxenhall. Glos 3D 51
Oxton. Mers 2D 9
Oxwich. Swan 3D 55
Oxwich Green. Swan 1A 62
Oystermouth. Swan 1B 62

P

Paddington. Warr 2D 11
Paddolgreen. Shrp 1C 27
Padeswood. Flin 1D 17
Painscastle. Powy 1C 49
Pale. Gwyn 1A 24
Palmerstown. V Glam 3C 65
Pandy. Gwyn 2D 23
 (nr. Bala)
Pandy. Gwyn 1B 28
 (nr. Tywyn)
Pandy. Mon 3A 50
Pandy. Powy 1A 30
Pandy. Wrex 1C 25
Pandy Tudur. Cnwy 1D 15
Pant. Shrp 2D 25
Pant. Wrex 3A 18
Pantasaph. Flin 3C 9
Pant Glas. Gwyn 3D 13
Pant-glas. Shrp 1D 25
Pantgwyn. Carm 3A 46
Pantgwyn. Cdgn 1B 44
Pant-lasau. Swan 3B 56
Pant-pastynog. Den 1B 16
Pantperthog. Gwyn 1C 29
Pant-teg. Carm 3D 45
Pant-y-Caws. Carm 3A 44
Pant-y-dwr. Powy 1A 38
Pant-y-ffridd. Powy 1C 31
Pantyffynnon. Carm 1B 56
Pantygasseg. Torf 2D 59
Pant-y-llyn. Carm 1B 56
Pant-yr-awel. B'end 1A 64
Pant y Wacco. Flin 3C 9
Parc. Gwyn 1D 23
Parcllyn. Cdgn 3B 34
Parc-Seymour. Newp 3B 60
Parkend. Glos 2D 61
Parkgate. Ches 3D 9
Park Hill. Mers 1B 10
Parkhouse. Mon 2B 60
Parkmill. Swan 1A 62
Parkway. Here 2D 51
Parr. Mers 1C 11
Parrog. Pemb 2D 43
Partington. G Man 2D 11
Patchway. S Glo 1D 67
Paulton. Bath 3D 67
Peasedown St John. Bath 3D 67
Peasley Cross. Mers 1C 11
Peaton. Shrp 3C 33
Peckforton. Ches 2C 19
Pedair-ffordd. Powy 2C 25
Pelcomb Bridge. Pemb 1C 53
Pelcomb Cross. Pemb 1C 53
Pemberton. Carm 2A 56
Pembrey. Carm 2D 55
Pembridge. Here 3A 40
Pembroke. Pemb 2C 53
Pembroke Dock. Pemb 2C 53
Pembroke Ferry. Pemb 2C 53
Penallt. Mon 2C 61
Penally. Pemb 3A 54
Penalt. Here 3C 51
Penalum. Pemb 3A 54
Penarth. V Glam 2C 65
Pen-bont Rhydybeddau. Cdgn 3B 28
Penbryn. Cdgn 3B 34
Pencader. Carm 2D 45
Pen-cae. Cdgn 3D 35
Pencaenewydd. Gwyn 3D 13
Pencaerau. Neat 3C 57
Pencarnisiog. IOA 3C 5
Pencarreg. Carm 1A 46
Pencelli. Powy 3B 48
Pen-clawdd. Swan 3A 56
Pencoed. B'end 1A 64
Pencombe. Here 3C 41
Pencraig. Here 3C 51
Pencraig. Powy 2B 24
Penderyn. Rhon 2A 58
Pendine. Carm 2B 54
Pendoylan. V Glam 2B 64

Pendre. B'end 1A 64
Penegoes. Powy 1C 29
Penffordd. Pemb 3D 43
Penffordd-Las. Powy 2D 29
Penfro. Pemb 2C 53
Pengam. Cphy 3C 59
Pengam. Card 2D 65
Pengenffordd. Powy 2C 49
Pengorffwysfa. IOA 1D 5
Pengwern. Den 3B 8
Penhelig. Gwyn 2B 28
Penhow. Newp 3B 60
Peniarth. Gwyn 1B 28
Peniel. Carm 3D 45
Penisa'r Waun. Gwyn 1A 14
Penketh. Warr 2C 11
Penley. Wrex 1B 26
Penllech. Gwyn 1B 20
Penllergaer. Swan 3B 56
Pen-llyn. IOA 2C 5
Penmachno. Cnwy 2C 15
Penmaen. Swan 1A 62
Penmaenmawr. Cnwy 3C 7
Penmaenpool. Gwyn 3B 22
Penmaen Rhos. Cnwy 3D 7
Penmark. V Glam 3B 64
Penmon. IOA 2B 6
Penmorfa. Gwyn 3A 14
Penmynydd. IOA 3A 6
Pennal. Gwyn 1C 29
Pennant. Cdgn 2A 36
Pennant. Den 1B 24
Pennant. Gwyn 2A 24
Pennant. Powy 2C 29
Pennant Melangell. Powy 2B 24
Pennar. Pemb 2C 53
Pennard. Swan 1A 62
Pennerley. Shrp 2A 32
Pennington. G Man 1D 11
Pennorth. Powy 3C 49
Pennsylvania. S Glo 2D 67
Penparc. Cdgn 1B 44
Penparcau. Cdgn 3A 28
Penpedairheol. Cphy 3C 59
Penperlleni. Mon 2A 60
Penpont. Powy 3A 48
Penprysg. B'end 1A 64
Penrherber. Carm 2B 44
Penrhiw. Pemb 1B 44
Penrhiwceiber. Rhon 3B 58
Pen Rhiwfawr. Neat 1C 57
Penrhiw-llan. Cdgn 1C 45
Penrhiw-pal. Cdgn 1C 45
Penrhos. Gwyn 1C 21
Penrhos. Here 3A 40
Penrhos. IOA 2B 4
Penrhos. Mon 1B 60
Penrhos. Powy 1D 57
Penrhos Garnedd. Gwyn 3A 6
Penrhyn. IOA 1C 5
Penrhyn Bay. Cnwy 2D 7
Penrhyn-coch. Cdgn 3B 28
Penrhyndeudraeth. Gwyn 1B 22
Penrhyn Side. Cnwy 2D 7
Penrice. Swan 3D 55
Pensarn. Carm 1D 55
Pen-sarn. Gwyn 2A 22
Pensax. Worc 2D 41
Pensby. Mers 2D 9
Pensford. Bath 3D 67
Pente-tafarn-y-fedw. Cnwy 1D 15
Pentir. Gwyn 1A 14
Pentlepoir. Pemb 2A 54
Pentraeth. IOA 3A 6
Pentre. Powy 2D 31
 (nr. Church Stoke)
Pentre. Powy 3C 31
 (nr. Kerry)
Pentre. Powy 3B 30
 (nr. Mochdre)
Pentre. Rhon 3A 58
Pentre. Shrp 3A 26
Pentre. Wrex 1C 25
 (nr. Llanfyllin)
Pentre. Wrex 3D 17
 (nr. Rhosllanerchrugog)
Pentrebach. Carm 2D 47
Pentre-bach. Cdgn 1A 46
Pentrebach. Mer T 2B 58
Pentre-bach. Powy 2A 48
Pentrebach. Swan 2B 56
Pentre Berw. IOA 3D 5
Pentre-bont. Cnwy 2C 15
Pentrecagal. Carm 1C 45
Pentre-celyn. Den 2C 17
Pentre-clawdd. Shrp 1D 25
Pentreclwydau. Neat 2D 57
Pentre-cwrt. Carm 2C 45
Pentre Dolau Honddu. Powy 1A 48

Pentre-du. Cnwy 2C 15
Pentre-dwr. Neat 3B 56
Pentrefelin. Carm 3A 46
Pentrefelin. Cdgn 1B 46
Pentrefelin. Cnwy 3D 7
Pentrefelin. Gwyn 1A 22
Pentrefoelas. Cnwy 2D 15
Pentre Galar. Pemb 2A 44
Pentregat. Cdgn 3C 35
Pentre Gwenlais. Carm 1B 56
Pentre Gwynfryn. Gwyn 2A 22
Pentre Halkyn. Flin 3D 9
Pentre Hodre. Shrp 1A 40
Pentre-Llanrhaeadr. Den 1B 16
Pentre Llifior. Powy 2C 31
Pentrellwyn. IOA 2A 6
Pentre-llwyn-llwyd. Powy 3A 38
Pentre-llyn-cymmer. Cnwy 2A 16
Pentre Meyrick. V Glam 2A 64
Pentre-piod. Gwyn 1D 23
Pentre-poeth. Newp 1D 65
Pentre'r Beirdd. Powy 3C 25
Pentre'r-felin. Powy 2A 48
Pentre-ty-gwyn. Carm 2D 47
Pentre-uchaf. Gwyn 1C 21
Pen-twyn. Cphy 2D 59
 (nr. Oakdale)
Pentwyn. Cphy 2C 59
 (nr. Rhymney)
Pentwyn. Card 1D 65
Pentyrch. Card 1C 65
Pentywyn. Carm 2B 54
Penuwch. Cdgn 2A 36
Penwyllt. Powy 1D 57
Penybanc. Carm 1B 56
 (nr. Ammanford)
Pen-y-banc. Carm 3B 46
 (nr. Llandeilo)
Pen-y-bont. Carm 3C 45
Penybont. Powy 2C 39
 (nr. Llandrindod Wells)
Pen-y-bont. Powy 2D 25
 (nr. Llanfyllin)
Pen-y-Bont Ar Ogwr. B'end 1A 64
Penybontfawr. Powy 2B 24
Penybryn. Cphy 3C 59
Pen-y-bryn. Pemb 1A 44
Pen-y-bryn. Wrex 3D 17
Pen-y-cae. Powy 1D 57
Penycae. Wrex 3D 17
Pen-y-cae-mawr. Mon 3B 60
Penycaerau. Gwyn 2A 20
Pen-y-cefn. Flin 3C 9
Pen-y-clawdd. Mon 2B 60
Pen-y-coedcae. Rhon 1B 64
Penycwm. Pemb 3B 42
Pen-y-darren. Mer T 2B 58
Pen-y-fai. B'end 1D 63
Penyffordd. Flin 1A 18
 (nr. Mold)
Pen-y-ffordd. Flin 3C 9
 (nr. Prestatyn)
Penyffridd. Gwyn 2A 14
Pen-y-garn. Cdgn 3B 28
Pen-y-garnedd. IOA 3A 6
Penygarnedd. Powy 2C 25
Pen-y-graig. Gwyn 1A 20
Penygraig. Rhon 3A 58
Pen-y-graigwen. IOA 2D 5
Pen-y-groes. Carm 1A 56
Penygroes. Gwyn 2D 13
Penygroes. Pemb 2A 44
Penymynydd. Flin 1A 18
Penyrheol. Cphy 1C 65
Pen-yr-heol. Mon 1B 60
Penyrheol. Swan 3A 56
Pen-yr-Heolgerrig. Mer T 2B 58
Penysarn. IOA 1D 5
Pen-y-stryt. Den 2D 17
Penywaun. Rhon 2A 58
Peplow. Shrp 2D 27
Perthy. Shrp 1A 26
Peterchurch. Here 2A 50
Peterstone Wentlooge.
 Newp 1D 65
Peterston-super-Ely.
 V Glam 2B 64
Peterstow. Here 3C 51
Petton. Shrp 2B 26
Phocle Green. Here 3D 51
Pibwrlwyd. Carm 1D 55
Picklenash. Glos 3D 51
Picklescott. Shrp 2B 32
Pickmere. Ches 3D 11
Pickstock. Telf 2D 27
Picton. Ches 3B 10
Picton. Flin 2C 9
Pie Corner. Here 2D 41
Pill. N Som 2C 67

Pilleth. *Powy* 2D **39**
Pillgwenlly. *Newp* 1A **66**
Pillowell. *Glos* 2D **61**
Pill, The. *Mon* 1B **66**
Pilning. *S Glo* 1C **67**
Pilton Green. *Swan* 3D **55**
Pinged. *Carm* 2D **55**
Pinsley Green. *Ches* 3C **19**
Pipe and Lyde. *Here* 1C **51**
Pipe Aston. *Here* 1B **40**
Pipe Gate. *Shrp* 3D **19**
Pipton. *Powy* 2C **49**
Pistyll. *Gwyn* 3C **13**
Pitchford. *Shrp* 1C **33**
Pitt Court. *Glos* 3D **61**
Pitton. *Swan* 3D **55**
Pixley. *Here* 2D **51**
Plain Dealings. *Pemb* 1D **53**
Plaish. *Shrp* 2C **33**
Plaistow. *Here* 1D **51**
Plas Llwyd. *Cnwy* 3A **8**
Plas yn Cefn. *Den* 3B **8**
Platt Bridge. *G Man* 1D **11**
Platt Lane. *Shrp* 1C **27**
Plealey. *Shrp* 1B **32**
Ploughfield. *Here* 1A **50**
Plowden. *Shrp* 3A **32**
Ploxgreen. *Shrp* 1A **32**
Plumley. *Ches* 3D **11**
Plwmp. *Cdgn* 3C **35**
Ponde. *Powy* 2C **49**
Pontamman. *Carm* 1B **56**
Pontantwn. *Carm* 1D **55**
Pontardawe. *Neat* 2C **57**
Pontardulais. *Swan* 2A **56**
Pontarfynach. *Cdgn* 1C **37**
Pont-ar-gothi. *Carm* 3A **46**
Pont ar Hydfer. *Powy* 3D **47**
Pontarllechau. *Carm* 3C **47**
Pontarsais. *Carm* 3D **45**
Pontblyddyn. *Flin* 1D **17**
Pontbren Llwyd. *Rhon* 2A **58**
Pont Cyfyng. *Cnwy* 2C **15**
Pontdolgoch. *Powy* 2B **30**
Ponterwyd. *Cdgn* 3C **29**
Pontesbury. *Shrp* 1B **32**
Pontesford. *Shrp* 1B **32**
Pontfadog. *Wrex* 1D **25**
Pontfaen. *Pemb* 2D **43**
Pont-faen. *Powy* 2A **48**
Pont-Faen. *Shrp* 1D **25**
Pontgarreg. *Cdgn* 3C **35**
Pont-Henri. *Carm* 2D **55**
Ponthir. *Torf* 3A **60**
Ponthirwaun. *Cdgn* 1B **44**
Pont-iets. *Carm* 2D **55**
Pontllanfraith. *Cphy* 3C **59**
Pontlliw. *Swan* 2B **56**
Pont Llogel. *Powy* 3B **24**
Pontllyfni. *Gwyn* 2D **13**
Pontlottyn. *Cphy* 2C **59**
Pontneddfechan. *Rhon* 2A **58**
Pont-newydd. *Carm* 2D **55**
Pont-newydd. *Flin* 1C **17**
Pontnewydd. *Torf* 3A **60**
Pont Pen-y-benglog.
   Gwyn 1B **14**
Pontrhydfendigaid. *Cdgn* 2C **37**
Pont Rhyd-y-cyff. *B'end* 1D **63**
Pontrhydyfen. *Neat* 3C **57**
Pont-rhyd-y-groes. *Cdgn* 1C **37**
Pontrhydyrun. *Torf* 3D **59**
Pont Rhythallt. *Gwyn* 1A **14**
Pontrilas. *Here* 3A **50**
Pontrilas Road. *Here* 3A **50**
Pontrobert. *Powy* 3C **25**
Pont-rug. *Gwyn* 1A **14**
Pontshill. *Here* 3D **51**
Pont-Sian. *Cdgn* 1D **45**
Pontsticill. *Mer T* 1B **58**
Pont-Walby. *Neat* 2D **57**
Pontwelly. *Carm* 2D **45**
Pontwgan. *Cnwy* 3C **7**
Pontyates. *Carm* 2D **55**
Pontyberem. *Carm* 1A **56**
Pontybodkin. *Flin* 2D **17**
Pontyclun. *Rhon* 1B **64**
Pontycymer. *B'end* 3A **58**
Pontyglazier. *Pemb* 2A **44**
Pontygwaith. *Rhon* 3B **58**
Pont-y-pant. *Cnwy* 2C **15**
Pontypool. *Torf* 3D **59**
Pontypridd. *Rhon* 3B **58**
Pontypwl. *Torf* 3D **59**
Pontywaun. *Cphy* 3D **59**
Poole Green. *Ches* 2D **19**
Pool Head. *Here* 3C **41**
Poolhill. *Glos* 3D **51**
Poolmill. *Here* 3C **51**

Pool Quay. *Powy* 3D **25**
Pope Hill. *Pemb* 1C **53**
Pope's Hill. *Glos* 1D **61**
Portbury. *N Som* 2C **67**
Port Dinorwig. *Gwyn* 1A **14**
Port-Eynon. *Swan* 1A **62**
Portfield Gate. *Pemb* 1C **53**
Porth. *Rhon* 3B **58**
Porthaethwy. *IOA* 3A **6**
Porthcawl. *B'end* 2D **63**
Porthgain. *Pemb* 2B **42**
Porthill. *Shrp* 3B **26**
Porthkerry. *V Glam* 3B **64**
Porthllechog. *IOA* 1D **5**
Porth Llechog. *IOA* 1D **5**
Porthmadog. *Gwyn* 1A **22**
Porthmeirion. *Gwyn* 1A **22**
Porth Tywyn. *Carm* 2D **55**
Porth-y-felin. *IOA* 2B **4**
Porthyrhyd. *Carm* 1A **56**
   (nr. Carmarthen)
Porthyrhyd. *Carm* 2D **47**
   (nr. Llandovery)
Porth-y-waen. *Shrp* 2D **25**
Portishead. *N Som* 2B **66**
Port Lion. *Pemb* 2C **53**
Port Mead. *Swan* 3B **56**
Portskewett. *Mon* 1C **67**
Port Sunlight. *Mers* 2A **10**
Port Talbot. *Neat* 1C **63**
Port Tennant. *Swan* 3B **56**
Portway. *Here* 1B **50**
Post-mawr. *Cdgn* 3D **35**
Pound Bank. *Worc* 1D **41**
Poynton. *Telf* 3C **27**
Poynton Green. *Telf* 3C **27**
Prees. *Shrp* 1C **27**
Prees Green. *Shrp* 1C **27**
Prees Higher Heath.
   Shrp 1C **27**
Prendergast. *Pemb* 1C **53**
Pren-gwyn. *Cdgn* 1D **45**
Prenteg. *Gwyn* 3A **14**
Prenton. *Mers* 2A **10**
Prescot. *Mers* 1B **10**
Prescott. *Shrp* 2B **26**
Prestatyn. *Den* 2B **8**
Presteigne. *Powy* 2A **40**
Presthope. *Shrp* 2C **33**
Preston. *Shrp* 3C **27**
Preston Brockhurst. *Shrp* 2C **27**
Preston Cross. *Glos* 2D **51**
Preston Gubbals. *Shrp* 3B **26**
Preston Marsh. *Here* 1C **51**
Preston on the Hill. *Hal* 2C **11**
Preston on Wye. *Here* 1A **50**
Preston upon the Weald Moors.
   Telf 3D **27**
Preston Wynne. *Here* 1C **51**
Price Town. *B'end* 3A **58**
Priest Weston. *Shrp* 2D **31**
Primrose Hill. *Glos* 2D **61**
Princes Gate. *Pemb* 1A **54**
Prion. *Den* 1B **16**
Prior's Frome. *Here* 2C **51**
Priors Halton. *Shrp* 1B **40**
Priorslee. *Telf* 3D **27**
Priory Wood. *Here* 1D **49**
Priston. *Bath* 3D **67**
Publow. *Bath* 3D **67**
Pucklechurch. *S Glo* 2D **67**
Puddinglake. *Ches* 1D **19**
Puddington. *Ches* 3A **10**
Puddlebrook. *Glos* 1D **61**
Pudleston. *Here* 3C **41**
Puleston. *Telf* 2D **27**
Pulford. *Ches* 2A **18**
Pulley. *Shrp* 1B **32**
Pulverbatch. *Shrp* 1B **32**
Pumpsaint. *Carm* 1B **46**
Puncheston. *Pemb* 3D **43**
Purlogue. *Shrp* 1D **39**
Purslow. *Shrp* 3A **32**
Purton. *Glos* 2D **61**
   (nr. Lydney)
Purton. *Glos* 2D **61**
   (nr. Sharpness)
Putley. *Here* 2D **51**
Puxton. *N Som* 3B **66**
Pwll. *Carm* 2D **55**
Pwll. *Powy* 1C **31**
Pwllcrochan. *Pemb* 2C **53**
Pwll-glas. *Den* 2C **17**
Pwllgloyw. *Powy* 2B **48**
Pwllheli. *Gwyn* 1C **21**
Pwllmeyric. *Mon* 3C **61**
Pwlltrap. *Carm* 1B **54**
Pwll-y-glaw. *Neat* 3C **57**

Pye Corner. *Newp* 1A **66**
Pyle. *Neat* 1D **63**

Q

Quabbs. *Shrp* 3D **31**
Quarrybank. *Ches* 1C **19**
Quarry, The. *Glos* 3D **61**
Quatford. *Shrp* 2D **33**
Queen Charlton. *Bath* 3D **67**
Queensferry. *Flin* 1A **18**
Quina Brook. *Shrp* 1C **27**

R

Raby. *Mers* 3A **10**
Rachub. *Gwyn* 1B **14**
Radford. *Bath* 3D **67**
Radyr. *Card* 1C **65**
Ragdon. *Shrp* 2B **32**
Raglan. *Mon* 2B **60**
Rainford. *Mers* 1B **10**
Rainford Junction. *Mers* 1B **10**
Rainhill. *Mers* 1B **10**
Rangeworthy. *S Glo* 1D **67**
Rassau. *Blae* 1C **59**
Ratlinghope. *Shrp* 2B **32**
Ravenhills Green. *Worc* 3D **41**
Ravensmoor. *Ches* 2D **19**
Rease Heath. *Ches* 2D **19**
Redberth. *Pemb* 2D **53**
Redbrook. *Mon* 1C **61**
Redbrook. *Wrex* 3C **19**
Redcliff Bay. *N Som* 2B **66**
Redhill. *N Som* 3B **66**
Redhill. *Shrp* 3D **27**
Redland. *Bris* 2C **67**
Redmarley D'Abitot.
   Glos 2D **51**
Rednal. *Shrp* 2A **26**
Red Roses. *Carm* 1B **54**
Red Wharf Bay. *IOA* 2A **6**
Redwick. *Newp* 1B **66**
Redwick. *S Glo* 1C **67**
Regil. *N Som* 3C **67**
Reilth. *Shrp* 3D **31**
Resolfen. *Neat* 2D **57**
Resolven. *Neat* 2D **57**
Reynalton. *Pemb* 2D **53**
Reynoldston. *Swan* 3D **55**
Rhadyr. *Mon* 2A **60**
Rhaeadr Gwy. *Powy* 2A **38**
Rhandirmwyn. *Carm* 1C **47**
Rhayader. *Powy* 2A **38**
Rhewl. *Den* 3C **17**
   (nr. Llangollen)
Rhewl. *Den* 1C **17**
   (nr. Ruthin)
Rhewl. *Shrp* 1A **26**
Rhewl-Mostyn. *Flin* 2C **9**
Rhigos. *Rhon* 2A **58**
Rhiw. *Gwyn* 2B **20**
Rhiwabon. *Wrex* 3A **18**
Rhiwbina. *Card* 1C **65**
Rhiwbryfdir. *Gwyn* 3B **14**
Rhiwderin. *Newp* 1D **65**
Rhiwlas. *Gwyn* 1A **24**
   (nr. Bala)
Rhiwlas. *Gwyn* 1A **14**
   (nr. Bangor)
Rhiwlas. *Powy* 1C **25**
Rhodiad-y-Brenin. *Pemb* 3A **42**
Rhondda. *Rhon* 1A **64**
Rhoose. *V Glam* 3B **64**
Rhos. *Carm* 2C **45**
Rhos. *Neat* 2C **57**
Rhosaman. *Carm* 1C **57**
Rhoscefnhir. *IOA* 3A **6**
Rhoscolyn. *IOA* 3B **4**
Rhos Common. *Powy* 3D **25**
Rhoscrowther. *Pemb* 2C **53**
Rhos-ddu. *Gwyn* 1B **20**
Rhosdylluan. *Gwyn* 2D **23**
Rhosesmor. *Flin* 1D **17**
Rhos-fawr. *Gwyn* 1C **21**
Rhosgadfan. *Gwyn* 2A **14**
Rhosgoch. *IOA* 2D **5**
Rhosgoch. *Powy* 1C **49**
Rhos Haminiog. *Cdgn* 2A **36**
Rhos-hill. *Pemb* 1A **44**
Rhoshirwaun. *Gwyn* 2A **20**
Rhoslan. *Gwyn* 3D **13**
Rhoslefain. *Gwyn* 1A **28**
Rhosllanerchrugog. *Wrex* 3D **17**
Rhos Lligwy. *IOA* 2D **5**
Rhosmaen. *Carm* 3B **46**
Rhosmeirch. *IOA* 3D **5**

Rhosneigr. *IOA* 3C **5**
Rhos-on-Sea. *Cnwy* 2D **7**
Rhossili. *Swan* 3D **55**
Rhosson. *Pemb* 3A **42**
Rhos, The. *Pemb* 1D **53**
Rhostrenwfa. *IOA* 3D **5**
Rhostryfan. *Gwyn* 2D **13**
Rhostyllen. *Wrex* 3A **18**
Rhoswiel. *Shrp* 1D **25**
Rhosybol. *IOA* 2D **5**
Rhos-y-brithdir. *Powy* 2C **25**
Rhos-y-garth. *Cdgn* 1B **36**
Rhos-y-gwaliau. *Gwyn* 1A **24**
Rhos-y-llan. *Gwyn* 1B **20**
Rhos-y-meirch. *Powy* 2D **39**
Rhuallt. *Den* 3B **8**
Rhuddall Heath. *Ches* 1C **19**
Rhuddlan. *Cdgn* 1D **45**
Rhuddlan. *Den* 3A **8**
Rhulen. *Powy* 1C **49**
Rhuthun. *Den* 2C **17**
Rhyd. *Gwyn* 3B **14**
Rhydaman. *Carm* 1B **56**
Rhydargaeau. *Carm* 3D **45**
Rhydcymerau. *Carm* 2A **14**
Rhyd-Ddu. *Gwyn* 2A **14**
Rhydding. *Neat* 3C **57**
Rhydfudr. *Cdgn* 2A **36**
Rhydlanfair. *Cnwy* 2D **15**
Rhydlewis. *Cdgn* 1C **45**
Rhydlios. *Gwyn* 1A **20**
Rhydlydan. *Cnwy* 2D **15**
Rhyd-meirionydd. *Cdgn* 3B **28**
Rhydowen. *Cdgn* 1D **45**
Rhyd-Rosser. *Cdgn* 2A **36**
Rhydspence. *Powy* 1D **49**
Rhydtalog. *Flin* 2D **17**
Rhyd-uchaf. *Gwyn* 1A **24**
Rhydwyn. *IOA* 2C **5**
Rhyd-y-clafdy. *Gwyn* 1C **21**
Rhydycroesau. *Shrp* 1D **25**
Rhydyfelin. *Cdgn* 1A **36**
Rhydyfelin. *Rhon* 1C **65**
Rhyd-y-foel. *Cnwy* 3A **8**
Rhyd-y-fro. *Neat* 2C **57**
Rhydymain. *Gwyn* 2D **23**
Rhyd-y-meirch. *Mon* 2A **60**
Rhyd-y-meudwy. *Den* 2C **17**
Rhydymwyn. *Flin* 1D **17**
Rhyd-yr-onen. *Gwyn* 1B **28**
Rhyd-y-sarn. *Gwyn* 3B **14**
Rhyl. *Den* 2B **8**
Rhymney. *Cphy* 2C **59**
Rhymni. *Cphy* 2C **59**
Richards Castle. *Here* 2B **40**
Rickford. *N Som* 3B **66**
Ridgebourne. *Powy* 3B **38**
Ridgeway Cross. *Here* 1D **51**
Ridgwardine. *Shrp* 1D **27**
Risbury. *Here* 3C **41**
Risca. *Cphy* 3D **59**
Risley. *Warr* 1D **11**
Roath. *Card* 2C **65**
Robertstown. *Rhon* 2A **58**
Robeston Back. *Pemb* 1D **53**
Robeston Wathen. *Pemb* 1D **53**
Robeston West. *Pemb* 2B **52**
Roch. *Pemb* 3B **42**
Rock. *Worc* 1D **41**
Rock Ferry. *Mers* 2A **10**
Rockfield. *Mon* 1B **60**
Rockgreen. *Shrp* 1C **41**
Rockhampton. *S Glo* 3D **61**
Rodd. *Here* 2A **40**
Roden. *Telf* 3C **27**
Rodington. *Telf* 3C **27**
Rodington Heath. *Telf* 3C **27**
Rodley. *Glos* 1D **61**
Rodway. *Telf* 3D **27**
Rogerstone. *Newp* 1D **65**
Rogiet. *Mon* 1B **66**
Roman Bank. *Shrp* 2C **33**
Romers Common. *Worc* 2C **41**
Rorrington. *Shrp* 1A **32**
Rosebush. *Pemb* 3D **43**
Rosehill. *Shrp* 1D **27**
   (nr. Market Drayton)
Rosehill. *Shrp* 3B **26**
   (nr. Shrewsbury)
Rosemarket. *Pemb* 2C **53**
Rossett. *Wrex* 2A **18**
Ross-on-Wye. *Here* 3D **51**
Rostherne. *Ches* 2D **11**
Round Oak. *Shrp* 3A **32**
Rowberrow. *Som* 3B **66**
Rowen. *Cnwy* 3C **7**
Rowley. *Shrp* 1A **32**
Rowlstone. *Here* 3A **50**
Rowton. *Ches* 1B **18**

Rowton. *Shrp* 3B **32**
(nr. Ludlow)
Rowton. *Shrp* 3A **26**
(nr. Shrewsbury)
Rowton. *Telf* 3D **27**
Royal's Green. *Ches* 3D **19**
Ruabon. *Wrex* 3A **18**
Ruardean. *Glos* 1D **61**
Ruardean Hill. *Glos* 1D **61**
Ruardean Woodside. *Glos* 1D **61**
Ruckley. *Shrp* 1C **33**
Rudbaxton. *Pemb* 3C **43**
Rudgeway. *S Glo* 1D **67**
Rudhall. *Here* 3D **51**
Rudheath. *Ches* 3D **11**
Rudheath Woods. *Ches* 3D **11**
Rudry. *Cphy* 1C **65**
Rumney. *Card* 2D **65**
Runcorn. *Hal* 2C **11**
Rushall. *Here* 2D **51**
Rushbury. *Shrp* 2C **33**
Rushton. *Ches* 1C **19**
Rushton. *Shrp* 1D **33**
Ruspidge. *Glos* 1D **61**
Ruthin. *Den* 2C **17**
Ruthin. *V Glam* 2A **64**
Ruxton Green. *Here* 1C **61**
Ruyton-XI-Towns. *Shrp* 2A **26**
Ryeford. *Here* 3D **51**
Ryton. *Glos* 2D **51**

S

Sageston. *Pemb* 2D **53**
Saighton. *Ches* 1B **18**
Sain Dunwyd. *V Glam* 3A **64**
Sain Hilari. *V Glam* 2B **64**
St Andrews Major. *V Glam* 2C **65**
St Arvans. *Mon* 3C **61**
St Asaph. *Den* 3B **8**
St Athan. *V Glam* 3B **64**
Sain Tathan. *V Glam* 3B **64**
St Briavels. *Glos* 2C **61**
St Brides. *Pemb* 1A **52**
St Bride's Major. *V Glam* 2D **63**
St Bride's Netherwent. *Mon* 1B **66**
St Bride's-super-Ely. *V Glam* 2B **64**
St Brides Wentlooge. *Newp* 1D **65**
St Clears. *Carm* 1B **54**
St David's. *Pemb* 3A **42**
St Dogmaels. *Pemb* 1A **44**
St Donat's. *V Glam* 3A **64**
St Fagans. *Card* 2C **65**
St Florence. *Pemb* 2D **53**
St George. *Cnwy* 3A **8**
St George's. *N Som* 3A **66**
St Georges. *V Glam* 2B **64**
St Harmon. *Powy* 1A **38**
St Helens. *Mers* 1B **10**
St Hilary. *V Glam* 2B **64**
St Illtyd. *Blae* 2D **59**
St Ishmael. *Carm* 2C **55**
St Ishmael's. *Pemb* 2B **52**
St Lythans. *V Glam* 2C **65**
St Margarets. *Here* 2A **50**
St Martin's. *Shrp* 1A **26**
St Mary Church. *V Glam* 2B **64**
St Mary Hill. *V Glam* 2A **64**
St Maughan's Green. *Mon* 1B **60**
St Mellons. *Card* 1D **65**
St Michaels. *Worc* 2C **41**
St Nicholas. *Pemb* 2C **43**
St Nicholas. *V Glam* 2B **64**
St Owen's Cross. *Here* 3C **51**
St Petrox. *Pemb* 3C **53**
St Thomas. *Swan* 3B **56**
St Twynnells. *Pemb* 3C **53**
St Weonards. *Here* 3B **50**
Salem. *Carm* 3B **46**
Salem. *Cdgn* 3B **28**
Salem. *Gwyn* 2A **14**
Salterswall. *Ches* 1D **19**
Saltford. *Bath* 3D **67**
Saltmead. *Card* 2C **65**
Saltney. *Flin* 1A **18**
Sambrook. *Telf* 2D **27**
Sandbach. *Ches* 1D **19**
Sandfields. *Neat* 3C **57**
Sandford. *N Som* 3B **66**
Sandford. *Shrp* 2A **26**
(nr. Oswestry)
Sandford. *Shrp* 1C **27**
(nr. Whitchurch)
Sandiway. *Ches* 3D **11**
Sandy. *Carm* 2D **55**
Sandycroft. *Flin* 1A **18**
Sandy Cross. *Here* 3D **41**
Sandy Haven. *Pemb* 2B **52**

Sandylane. *Swan* 1A **62**
Sandyway. *Here* 3B **50**
Sapey Common. *Here* 2D **41**
Sardis. *Carm* 2A **56**
Sardis. *Pemb* 2C **53**
(nr. Milford Haven)
Sardis. *Pemb* 2A **54**
(nr. Tenby)
Sarn. *B'end* 1A **64**
Sarn. *Powy* 2D **31**
Sarnau. *Carm* 3D **45**
Sarnau. *Cdgn* 3C **35**
Sarnau. *Gwyn* 1A **24**
Sarnau. *Powy* 2B **48**
(nr. Brecon)
Sarnau. *Powy* 3D **25**
(nr. Welshpool)
Sarn Bach. *Gwyn* 2C **21**
Sarnesfield. *Here* 3A **40**
Sarn Meyllteyrn. *Gwyn* 1B **20**
Saron. *Carm* 1B **56**
(nr. Ammanford)
Saron. *Carm* 2C **45**
(nr. Newcastle Emlyn)
Saron. *Gwyn* 1A **14**
(nr. Bethel)
Saron. *Gwyn* 1D **15**
(nr. Bontnewydd)
Saughall. *Ches* 3A **10**
Saul. *Glos* 2D **61**
Saundersfoot. *Pemb* 2A **54**
Scethrog. *Powy* 3C **49**
School Green. *Ches* 1D **19**
Scleddau. *Pemb* 2C **43**
Scolton. *Pemb* 3C **43**
Scurlage. *Swan* 3D **55**
Seacombe. *Mers* 1A **10**
Seaforth. *Mers* 1A **10**
Sealand. *Flin* 1A **18**
Sea Mills. *Bris* 2C **67**
Sebastopol. *Cphy* 2C **59**
Sebastopol. *Torf* 3D **59**
Sedbury. *Glos* 3C **61**
Sefton. *Mers* 1A **10**
Sefton Park. *Mers* 2A **10**
Seifton. *Shrp* 3B **32**
Selattyn. *Shrp* 1D **25**
Sellack. *Here* 3C **51**
Senghenydd. *Cphy* 3C **59**
Sennybridge. *Powy* 3A **48**
Seven Sisters. *Neat* 2D **57**
Severn Beach. *S Glo* 1C **67**
Shakesfield. *Glos* 2D **51**
Sharpness. *Glos* 2D **61**
Shavington. *Ches* 2D **19**
Shawbirch. *Telf* 3D **27**
Shawbury. *Shrp* 2C **27**
Sheepway. *N Som* 2B **66**
Sheinton. *Shrp* 1D **33**
Shelderton. *Shrp* 1B **40**
Shell Green. *Hal* 2C **11**
Shelsey Beauchamp. *Worc* 2D **41**
Shelsley Walsh. *Worc* 2D **41**
Shelton. *Shrp* 3B **26**
Shelve. *Shrp* 2A **32**
Shelwick. *Here* 1C **51**
Shelwick Green. *Here* 1C **51**
Shenmore. *Here* 2A **50**
Shepperdine. *S Glo* 3D **61**
Shifnal. *Shrp* 1D **33**
Shipham. *Som* 3B **66**
Shipton. *Shrp* 2C **33**
Shirehampton. *Bris* 2C **67**
Shirenewton. *Mon* 3B **60**
Shirl Heath. *Here* 3B **40**
Shobdon. *Here* 2A **40**
Shocklach. *Ches* 3B **18**
Shoot Hill. *Shrp* 3B **26**
Shortwood. *S Glo* 2D **67**
Shoscombe. *Bath* 3D **67**
Shotton. *Flin* 1D **17**
Shotwick. *Ches* 3A **10**
Shrawardine. *Shrp* 3A **26**
Shrewsbury. *Shrp* 3B **26**
Shucknall. *Here* 1C **51**
Sibdon Carwood. *Shrp* 3B **32**
Sidbury. *Shrp* 3D **33**
Sidcot. *N Som* 3B **66**
Sigingstone. *V Glam* 2A **64**
Silian. *Cdgn* 3A **36**
Silvington. *Shrp* 3D **33**
Simm's Cross. *Hal* 2C **11**
Simm's Lane End. *Mers* 1C **11**
Simpson. *Pemb* 1B **52**
Simpson Cross. *Pemb* 1B **52**
Sirhowy. *Blae* 1C **59**
Siston. *S Glo* 2D **67**
Six Bells. *Blae* 2D **59**
Skenfrith. *Mon* 3B **50**

Sketty. *Swan* 3B **56**
Skewen. *Neat* 3C **57**
Skyborry Green. *Shrp* 1D **39**
Slade. *Swan* 1A **62**
Sleap. *Shrp* 2B **26**
Slimbridge. *Glos* 2D **61**
Smithies, The. *Shrp* 2D **33**
Smithy Green. *Ches* 3D **11**
Snailbeach. *Shrp* 1A **32**
Snead. *Powy* 2A **32**
Snead Common. *Worc* 2D **41**
Snitton. *Shrp* 1C **41**
Snodhill. *Here* 1A **50**
Soar. *Carm* 3B **46**
Soar. *Gwyn* 1B **22**
Soar. *IOA* 3C **5**
Soar. *Powy* 2A **48**
Sodom. *Den* 3B **8**
Sollers Dilwyn. *Here* 3B **40**
Sollers Hope. *Here* 2D **51**
Solva. *Pemb* 3A **42**
Soudley. *Shrp* 2B **32**
(nr. Church Stretton)
Soudley. *Shrp* 2D **27**
(nr. Market Drayton)
Soughton. *Flin* 1D **17**
Soundwell. *S Glo* 2D **67**
South Cornelly. *B'end* 1D **63**
Southdown. *Bath* 3D **67**
Southend. *Glos* 3D **61**
Southerndown. *V Glam* 2D **63**
Southgate. *Cdgn* 3A **28**
Southgate. *Swan* 1A **62**
Southstoke. *Bath* 3D **67**
South Widcombe. *Bath* 3C **67**
Speke. *Mers* 2B **10**
Spital. *Mers* 2A **10**
Spittal. *Pemb* 3C **43**
Sproston Green. *Ches* 1D **19**
Spurstow. *Ches* 2C **19**
Stackpole. *Pemb* 3C **53**
Stackpole Elidor. *Pemb* 3C **53**
Stafford Park. *Telf* 1D **33**
Stamford Bridge. *Ches* 1B **18**
Standford Bridge. *Telf* 2D **27**
Stanford Bishop. *Here* 1D **51**
Stanford Bridge. *Worc* 2D **41**
Stanford on Teme. *Worc* 2D **41**
Stanley. *Shrp* 3D **33**
Stanley Hill. *Here* 1D **51**
Stanlow. *Ches* 3B **10**
Stansbatch. *Here* 2A **40**
Stanthorne. *Ches* 1D **19**
Stanton Drew. *Bath* 3C **67**
Stanton Lacy. *Shrp* 1B **40**
Stanton Long. *Shrp* 2C **33**
Stanton Prior. *Bath* 3D **67**
Stanton upon Hine Heath. *Shrp* . . .2C **27**
Stanton Wick. *Bath* 3D **67**
Stanwardine in the Fields. *Shrp* . . .2B **26**
Stanwardine in the Wood. *Shrp* . . .2B **26**
Stapeley. *Ches* 3D **19**
Staple Hill. *S Glo* 2D **67**
Stapleton. *Bris* 2D **67**
Stapleton. *Here* 2A **40**
Stapleton. *Shrp* 1B **32**
Staplow. *Here* 1D **51**
Star. *Pemb* 2B **44**
Staunton. *Glos* 1C **61**
Staunton on Arrow. *Here* 2A **40**
Staunton on Wye. *Here* 1A **50**
Staylittle. *Powy* 2D **29**
Steel Heath. *Shrp* 1C **27**
Steen's Bridge. *Here* 3C **41**
Stepaside. *Pemb* 2A **54**
Steynton. *Pemb* 2C **53**
Stifford's Bridge. *Here* 1D **51**
Stinchcombe. *Glos* 3D **61**
Stiperstones. *Shrp* 1A **32**
Stirchley. *Telf* 1D **33**
Stoak. *Ches* 3B **10**
Stocking. *Here* 2D **51**
Stockton. *Here* 2C **41**
Stockton. *Shrp* 2D **33**
(nr. Bridgnorth)
Stockton. *Shrp* 1D **31**
(nr. Chirbury)
Stockton Cross. *Here* 2C **41**
Stockton Heath. *Warr* 2D **11**
Stockton on Teme. *Worc* 2D **41**
Stockwood. *Bris* 3D **67**
Stoke Bliss. *Worc* 2D **41**
Stoke Cross. *Here* 3D **41**
Stoke Edith. *Here* 1D **51**
Stoke Gifford. *S Glo* 2D **67**
Stoke Heath. *Shrp* 2D **27**
Stoke Lacy. *Here* 1D **51**
Stoke on Tern. *Shrp* 2D **27**
Stoke Prior. *Here* 3C **41**

Stokesay. *Shrp* 3B **32**
Stoke St Milborough. *Shrp* 3C **33**
Stone. *Glos* 3D **61**
Stoneacton. *Shrp* 2C **33**
Stonebridge. *N Som* 3A **66**
Stone-edge-Batch. *N Som* 2B **66**
Stoneley Green. *Ches* 2D **19**
Stoney Stretton. *Shrp* 1A **32**
Stony Cross. *Here* 1D **51**
(nr. Great Malvern)
Stony Cross. *Here* 2C **41**
(nr. Leominster)
Storeton. *Mers* 2A **10**
Storridge. *Here* 1D **51**
Stottesdon. *Shrp* 3D **33**
Stowe. *Glos* 2C **61**
Stowe. *Shrp* 1A **40**
Stowey. *Bath* 3C **67**
Strangford. *Here* 3C **51**
Strata Florida. *Cdgn* 2C **37**
Street Dinas. *Shrp* 1A **26**
Strefford. *Shrp* 3B **32**
Stretford. *Here* 3C **41**
Stretton. *Ches* 2B **18**
Stretton. *Warr* 2D **11**
Stretton Grandison. *Here* 1D **51**
Stretton Heath. *Shrp* 3A **26**
Stretton Sugwas. *Here* 1B **50**
Stretton Westwood. *Shrp* 2C **33**
Stroat. *Glos* 3C **61**
Stryd. *IOA* 2B **4**
Stryt-issa. *Wrex* 3D **17**
Suckley. *Worc* 3D **41**
Suckley Knowl. *Worc* 3D **41**
Sudbrook. *Mon* 1C **67**
Sugwas Pool. *Here* 1B **50**
Sully. *V Glam* 3C **65**
Summerhill. *Pemb* 2A **54**
Sutton. *Pemb* 1C **53**
Sutton. *Shrp* 3D **33**
(nr. Bridgnorth)
Sutton. *Shrp* 1D **27**
(nr. Market Drayton)
Sutton. *Shrp* 2A **26**
(nr. Oswestry)
Sutton. *Shrp* 3C **27**
(nr. Shrewsbury)
Sutton. *Worc* 2D **41**
Sutton Leach. *Mers* 1C **11**
Sutton Maddock. *Shrp* 1D **33**
Sutton St Michael. *Here* 1C **51**
Sutton St Nicholas. *Here* 1C **51**
Sutton Weaver. *Ches* 3C **11**
Swainshill. *Here* 1B **50**
Swanbridge. *V Glam* 3C **65**
Swan Green. *Ches* 3D **11**
Swansea. *Swan* 3B **56**
Swanwick Green. *Ches* 2D **19**
Sweet Green. *Worc* 2D **41**
Swffyrd. *Cphy* 3D **59**
Swineford. *S Glo* 3D **67**
Swinmore Common. *Here* 1D **51**
Sworton Heath. *Ches* 2D **11**
Swydffynnon. *Cdgn* 2B **36**
Swyffrd. *Cphy* 3D **59**
Sycharth. *Powy* 2D **25**
Sychdyn. *Flin* 1D **17**
Sychnant. *Powy* 1A **38**
Sychtyn. *Powy* 1A **30**
Sydney. *Ches* 2D **19**
Sylen. *Carm* 2A **56**
Sylfaen. *Powy* 1C **31**
Symonds Yat. *Here* 1C **61**
Synod Inn. *Cdgn* 3D **35**

T

Tadwick. *Bath* 2D **67**
Tafarnaubach. *Cphy* 1C **59**
Tafarn-y-bwlch. *Pemb* 2D **43**
Tafarn-y-Gelyn. *Den* 1C **17**
Taff's Well. *Card* 1C **65**
Tafolwern. *Powy* 1D **29**
Taibach. *Neat* 1C **63**
Tai-bach. *Powy* 2C **25**
Tai-Nant. *Wrex* 3D **17**
Tai'n Lon. *Gwyn* 2D **13**
Tairgwaith. *Neat* 1C **57**
Talachddu. *Powy* 2B **48**
Talacre. *Flin* 2C **9**
Talardd. *Gwyn* 2D **23**
Talbenny. *Pemb* 1B **52**
Talbot Green. *Rhon* 1B **64**
Talerddig. *Powy* 1A **30**
Talgarreg. *Cdgn* 3D **35**
Talgarth. *Powy* 2C **49**
Tallarn Green. *Wrex* 3B **18**
Talley. *Carm* 2B **46**

Talog. *Carm* 3C 45
Talsarn. *Carm* 3C 47
Talsarn. *Cdgn* 3A 36
Talsarnau. *Gwyn* 1B 22
Talwrn. *IOA* 3D 5
Talwrn. *Wrex* 3D 17
Tal-y-bont. *Cdgn* 3B 28
Tal-y-Bont. *Cnwy* 1C 15
Tal-y-bont. *Gwyn* 3B 6
(nr. Bangor)
Tal-y-bont. *Gwyn* 2A 22
(nr. Barmouth)
Talybont-on-Usk. *Powy* 3C 49
Tal-y-cafn. *Cnwy* 3C 7
Tal-y-coed. *Mon* 1B 60
Tal-y-llyn. *Gwyn* 1C 29
Talyllyn. *Powy* 3C 49
Talysarn. *Gwyn* 2D 13
Tal-y-waenydd. *Gwyn* 3B 14
Talywain. *Torf* 2D 59
Talywern. *Powy* 1D 29
Tanerdy. *Carm* 3D 45
Tangiers. *Pemb* 1C 53
Tan-lan. *Cnwy* 1C 15
Tan-lan. *Gwyn* 3B 14
Tan-y-bwlch. *Gwyn* 3B 14
Tan-y-fron. *Cnwy* 1A 16
Tanyfron. *Wrex* 2D 17
Tan-y-goes. *Cdgn* 1B 44
Tanygrisiau. *Gwyn* 3B 14
Tan-y-pistyll. *Powy* 2B 24
Tan-yr-allt. *Den* 2B 8
Tarbock Green. *Mers* 2B 10
Tarporley. *Ches* 1C 19
Tarrington. *Here* 1D 51
Tarvin. *Ches* 1B 18
Tasley. *Shrp* 2D 33
Tattenhall. *Ches* 2B 18
Tavernspite. *Pemb* 1A 54
Taynton. *Glos* 3D 51
Tedsmore. *Shrp* 2A 26
Tedstone Delamere. *Here* 3D 41
Tedstone Wafer. *Here* 3D 41
Tegryn. *Pemb* 2B 44
Telford. *Telf* 3D 27
Temple Bar. *Carm* 1A 56
Temple Bar. *Cdgn* 3A 36
Temple Cloud. *Bath* 3D 67
Templeton. *Pemb* 1A 54
Tenbury Wells. *Worc* 2C 41
Tenby. *Pemb* 2A 54
Terfyn. *Cnwy* 3A 8
Ternhill. *Shrp* 1D 27
Tetchill. *Shrp* 1A 26
Thatto Heath. *Mers* 1C 11
Thelwall. *Warr* 2D 11
Thingwall. *Mers* 2D 9
Thomas Chapel. *Pemb* 2A 54
Thomastown. *Rhon* 1B 64
Thorn. *Powy* 2D 39
Thornbury. *Here* 3D 41
Thornbury. *S Glo* 1D 67
Thornhill. *Cphy* 1C 65
Thornton. *Mers* 1A 10
Thornton Hough. *Mers* 2A 10
Thornton-le-Moors. *Ches* 3B 10
Threapwood. *Ches* 3B 18
Three Ashes. *Here* 3C 51
Three Cocks. *Powy* 2C 49
Three Crosses. *Swan* 3A 56
Thruxton. *Here* 2B 50
Thurstaston. *Mers* 2D 9
Tibberton. *Telf* 2D 27
Tickenham. *N Som* 2B 66
Ticklerton. *Shrp* 2B 32
Tidenham. *Glos* 3C 61
Tiers Cross. *Pemb* 1C 53
Tillers Green. *Glos* 2D 51
Tilley. *Shrp* 2C 27
Tillington. *Here* 1B 50
Tillington Common. *Here* 1B 50
Tilstock. *Shrp* 1C 27
Tilston. *Ches* 2B 18
Tilstone Fearnall. *Ches* 1C 19
Timsbury. *Bath* 3D 67
Tintern Parva. *Mon* 2C 61
Tirabad. *Powy* 1D 47
Tircoed. *Swan* 2B 56
Tirnewydd. *Flin* 3C 9
Tirphil. *Cphy* 2C 59
Tir-y-dail. *Carm* 1B 56
Titley. *Here* 3A 40
Tiverton. *Ches* 1C 19
Tockington. *S Glo* 1D 67
Todding. *Here* 1B 40
Ton. *Mon* 3A 60
Tondu. *B'end* 1D 63
Tonfanau. *Gwyn* 1A 28
Tongwynlais. *Card* 1C 65

Tonmawr. *Neat* 3D 57
Tonna. *Neat* 3C 57
Ton-Pentre. *Rhon* 3A 58
Tonypandy. *Rhon* 3A 58
Tonyrefail. *Rhon* 1B 64
Tortworth. *S Glo* 3D 61
Tower Hill. *Mers* 1B 10
Town End. *Mers* 2B 10
Townhill. *Swan* 3B 56
Towyn. *Cnwy* 3A 8
Toxteth. *Mers* 2A 10
Trallong. *Powy* 3A 48
Tranmere. *Mers* 2A 10
Trapp. *Carm* 1B 56
Trawscoed. *Powy* 2B 48
Trawsfynydd. *Gwyn* 1C 23
Trawsgoed. *Cdgn* 1B 36
Treaddow. *Here* 3C 51
Trealaw. *Rhon* 3B 58
Trearddur. *IOA* 3B 4
Trebanog. *Rhon* 3B 58
Trebanos. *Neat* 2C 57
Trecastle. *Powy* 3D 47
Trecenydd. *Cphy* 1C 65
Trecwn. *Pemb* 2C 43
Trecynon. *Rhon* 2A 58
Tredegar. *Blae* 2C 59
Trederwen. *Powy* 3D 25
Tredogan. *V Glam* 3B 64
Tredomen. *Powy* 2C 49
Tredunnock. *Mon* 3A 60
Tredustan. *Powy* 2C 49
Trefaldwyn. *Powy* 2D 31
Trefasser. *Pemb* 2B 42
Trefdraeth. *IOA* 3D 5
Trefdraeth. *Pemb* 2D 43
Trefecca. *Powy* 2C 49
Trefechan. *Mer T* 2B 58
Trefeglwys. *Powy* 2A 30
Trefeitha. *Powy* 2C 49
Trefenter. *Cdgn* 1B 36
Treffgarne. *Pemb* 3C 43
Treffynnon. *Flin* 3C 9
Treffynnon. *Pemb* 3B 42
Trefil. *Blae* 1C 59
Trefilan. *Cdgn* 3A 36
Trefin. *Pemb* 2B 42
Treflach. *Shrp* 2D 25
Trefnant. *Den* 3B 8
Trefonen. *Shrp* 2D 25
Trefor. *Gwyn* 3C 13
Trefor. *IOA* 3C 5
Treforest. *Rhon* 1B 64
Trefriw. *Cnwy* 1C 15
Tref-y-Clawdd. *Powy* 1D 39
Trefynwy. *Mon* 1C 61
Tregare. *Mon* 1B 60
Tregaron. *Cdgn* 3B 36
Tregarth. *Gwyn* 1B 14
Tregeiriog. *Wrex* 1C 25
Tregele. *IOA* 1C 5
Tregolwyn. *V Glam* 2A 64
Tregoyd. *Powy* 2C 49
Tre-groes. *Cdgn* 1D 45
Tregynon. *Powy* 2B 30
Trehafod. *Rhon* 3B 58
Treharris. *Mer T* 3C 59
Treherbert. *Rhon* 3A 58
Trelales. *B'end* 1D 63
Trelawnyd. *Flin* 3B 8
Trelech. *Carm* 2B 44
Treleddyd-fawr. *Pemb* 3A 42
Trelewis. *Mer T* 3C 59
Trelleck. *Mon* 2C 61
Trelleck Grange. *Mon* 2B 60
Trelogan. *Flin* 2C 9
Trelystan. *Powy* 1D 31
Tremadog. *Gwyn* 3A 14
Tremain. *Cdgn* 1B 44
Tremeirchion. *Den* 3B 8
Tremorfa. *Card* 2D 65
Trench. *Telf* 3D 27
Treoes. *V Glam* 2A 64
Treorchy. *Rhon* 3A 58
Treorci. *Rhon* 3A 58
Tre'r-ddol. *Cdgn* 2B 28
Tre'r llai. *Powy* 1D 31
Tresaith. *Cdgn* 3B 34
Tresigin. *V Glam* 2A 64
Tresimwn. *V Glam* 2B 64
Tre Taliesin. *Cdgn* 2B 28
Trethomas. *Cphy* 1C 65
Tretio. *Pemb* 3A 42
Tretire. *Here* 3C 51
Tretower. *Powy* 3C 49
Treuddyn. *Flin* 2D 17
Trevalyn. *Wrex* 2A 18
Tre-vaughan. *Carm* 3D 45
(nr. Carmarthen)

Trevaughan. *Carm* 1A 54
(nr. Whitland)
Trevethin. *Torf* 2D 59
Trevor. *Den* 3D 17
Trevor Uchaf. *Den* 3D 17
Trewern. *Powy* 3D 25
Trewyddel. *Pemb* 1A 44
Trimsaran. *Carm* 2D 55
Trinant. *Cphy* 3D 59
Trisant. *Cdgn* 1C 37
Troedrhiwdalar. *Powy* 3A 38
Troedrhiwfuwch. *Cphy* 2C 59
Troedrhiwgwair. *Blae* 2C 59
Troedyraur. *Cdgn* 1C 45
Troedyrhiw. *Mer T* 2B 58
Trumpet. *Here* 2D 51
Tryfil. *IOA* 2D 5
Tudorville. *Here* 3C 51
Tudweiliog. *Gwyn* 1B 20
Tufton. *Pemb* 3D 43
Tugford. *Shrp* 3C 33
Tumble. *Carm* 1A 56
Tunley. *Bath* 3D 67
Tupsley. *Here* 1C 51
Turnant. *Here* 3A 50
Turnastone. *Here* 2A 50
Tutshill. *Glos* 3C 61
Tweedale. *Telf* 1D 33
Twerton. *Bath* 3D 67
Twinhoe. *Bath* 3D 67
Twiss Green. *Warr* 1D 11
Twitchen. *Shrp* 1A 40
Two Bridges. *Glos* 2D 61
Twyford Common. *Here* 2C 51
Twyncarno. *Cphy* 2C 59
Twynllanan. *Carm* 3C 47
Twynmynydd. *Carm* 1B 56
Twyn-y-Sheriff. *Mon* 2B 60
Tyberton. *Here* 2A 50
Tycroes. *Carm* 1B 56
Tycrwyn. *Powy* 3C 25
Tyddewi. *Pemb* 3A 42
Ty Issa. *Powy* 1C 25
Tyldesley. *G Man* 1D 11
Tyle. *Carm* 3B 46
Tylorstown. *Rhon* 3B 58
Tylwch. *Powy* 3A 30
Ty-nant. *Cnwy* 3A 16
Tynewydd. *Rhon* 3A 58
Ty'n-y-bryn. *Rhon* 1B 64
Tyn-y-celyn. *Wrex* 1C 25
Tyn-y-cwm. *Swan* 2B 56
Tyn-y-ffridd. *Powy* 1C 25
Tynygongl. *IOA* 2A 6
Tynygraig. *Cdgn* 2B 36
Tyn-y-groes. *Cnwy* 3C 7
Ty'n-yr-eithin. *Cdgn* 2B 36
Tyn-y-rhyd. *Powy* 3B 24
Tyn-y-wern. *Powy* 2B 24
Tythegston. *B'end* 2D 63
Tytherington. *S Glo* 1D 67
Tywyn. *Cnwy* 3C 7
Tywyn. *Gwyn* 1A 28

U

Ubley. *Bath* 3C 67
Uckington. *Shrp* 1C 33
Uffington. *Shrp* 3C 27
Uldingswick. *Here* 1C 51
Underdale. *Shrp* 3C 27
Underton. *Shrp* 2D 33
Undy. *Mon* 1B 66
Upcott. *Here* 3A 40
Uphampton. *Here* 2A 40
Uphill. *N Som* 3A 66
Upleadon. *Glos* 3D 51
Upper Affcot. *Shrp* 3B 32
Upper Bangor. *Gwyn* 3A 6
Upper Borth. *Cdgn* 3B 28
Upper Breinton. *Here* 1B 50
Upper Brynamman. *Carm* 1C 57
Upper Chapel. *Powy* 1B 48
Upper Church Village. *Rhon* 1B 64
Upper Coedcae. *Torf* 2D 59
Upper Cound. *Shrp* 1C 33
Upper Cwmbran. *Torf* 3D 59
Upper Dinchope. *Shrp* 3B 32
Upper Framilode. *Glos* 1D 61
Upper Grove Common. *Here* 3C 51
Upper Hardwick. *Here* 3B 40
Upper Hayton. *Shrp* 3C 33
Upper Heath. *Shrp* 3C 33
Upper Hengoed. *Shrp* 1D 25
Upper Hergest. *Here* 3D 39
Upper Hill. *Here* 3B 40
Upper Killay. *Swan* 3A 56
Upper Langford. *N Som* 3B 66

Upper Longwood. *Shrp* 1D 33
Upper Lydbrook. *Glos* 1D 61
Upper Lye. *Here* 2A 40
Upper Maes-coed. *Here* 2A 50
Upper Millichope. *Shrp* 3C 33
Upper Nash. *Pemb* 2D 53
Upper Netchwood. *Shrp* 2D 33
Upper Rochford. *Worc* 2D 41
Upper Sapey. *Here* 2D 41
Upper Soudley. *Glos* 1D 61
Upper Town. *Here* 1C 51
Upper Town. *N Som* 3C 67
Uppington. *Shrp* 1C 33
Upton. *Ches* 1B 18
Upton. *Mers* 2D 9
Upton. *Pemb* 2D 53
Upton Bishop. *Here* 3D 51
Upton Cheyney. *S Glo* 3D 67
Upton Cressett. *Shrp* 2D 33
Upton Crews. *Here* 3D 51
Upton Heath. *Ches* 1B 18
Upton Magna. *Shrp* 3C 27
Urdimarsh. *Here* 1C 51
Urmston. *G Man* 1C 11
Usk. *Mon* 2A 60
Uwchmynydd. *Gwyn* 2A 20
Uzmaston. *Pemb* 1C 53

V

Valley. *IOA* 3B 4
Van. *Powy* 3A 30
Varteg. *Torf* 2D 59
Vauld,The. *Here* 1C 51
Vaynol. *Gwyn* 3A 6
Vaynor. *Mer T* 1B 58
Velindre. *Powy* 2C 49
Vennington. *Shrp* 1A 32
Venn's Green. *Here* 1C 51
Vernolds Common. *Shrp* 3B 32
Viney Hill. *Glos* 2D 61
Vowchurch. *Here* 2A 50
Vulcan Village. *Warr* 1C 11

W

Waddicar. *Mers* 1A 10
Waen. *Den* 1B 16
(nr. Bodfari)
Waen. *Den* 1C 17
(nr. Llandyrnog)
Waen. *Den* 1A 16
(nr. Nantglyn)
Waen. *Powy* 2A 30
Waen Fach. *Powy* 3D 25
Waen Goleugoed. *Den* 3B 8
Walcot. *Telf* 3C 27
Walford. *Here* 1A 40
(nr. Leintwardine)
Walford. *Here* 3C 51
(nr. Ross-on-Wye)
Walford. *Shrp* 2B 26
Walford Heath. *Shrp* 3B 26
Walgherton. *Ches* 3D 19
Walkden. *G Man* 1D 11
Walker's Green. *Here* 1C 51
Wallasey. *Mers* 1A 10
Wallaston Green. *Pemb* 2C 53
Wallis. *Pemb* 3D 43
Wall under Heywood. *Shrp* 2C 33
Walterston. *V Glam* 2B 64
Walterstone. *Here* 3A 50
Walton. *Mers* 1A 10
Walton. *Powy* 3D 39
Walton. *Telf* 3C 27
Walton East. *Pemb* 3D 43
Walton-in-Gordano. *N Som* 2B 66
Walton West. *Pemb* 1B 52
Walwyn's Castle. *Pemb* 1B 52
Wanswell. *Glos* 2D 61
Wapley. *S Glo* 2D 67
Warburton. *G Man* 2D 11
Wardle. *Ches* 2D 19
Warmingham. *Ches* 1D 19
Warmley. *S Glo* 2D 67
Warren. *Pemb* 3C 53
Warrington. *Warr* 2D 11
Waterloo. *Cphy* 1C 65
Waterloo. *Here* 1A 50
Waterloo. *Mers* 1A 10
Waterloo. *Pemb* 2C 53
Waterloo. *Shrp* 1B 26
Waterston. *Pemb* 2C 53
Waters Upton. *Telf* 3D 27
Wattlesborough Heath. *Shrp* 3A 26
Wattstown. *Rhon* 3B 58
Wattsville. *Cphy* 3D 59

Waun. *Powy* 3D **25**
Waunarlwydd. *Swan* 3B **56**
Waun Fawr. *Cdgn* 3A **28**
Waunfawr. *Gwyn* 2A **14**
Waungilwen. *Carm* 2C **45**
Waunlwyd. *Blae* 2C **59**
Waun-y-Clyn. *Carm* 2D **55**
Waverton. *Ches* 1B **18**
Wavertree. *Mers* 2A **10**
Wdig. *Pemb* 2C **43**
Weaverham. *Ches* 3D **11**
Webton. *Here* 2B **50**
Wellington. *Here* 1B **50**
Wellington. *Telf* 3D **27**
Wellington Heath. *Here* 1D **51**
Wellow. *Bath* 3D **67**
Wells Green. *Ches* 2D **19**
Welshampton. *Shrp* 1B **26**
Welsh End. *Shrp* 1C **27**
Welsh Frankton. *Shrp* 1A **26**
Welsh Hook. *Pemb* 3C **43**
Welsh Newton. *Here* 1B **60**
Welsh Newton Common. *Here* 1C **61**
Welshpool. *Powy* 1D **31**
Welsh St Donats. *V Glam* 2B **64**
Wem. *Shrp* 2C **27**
Wenallt. *Cdgn* 1B **36**
Wenallt. *Gwyn* 3A **16**
Wentnor. *Shrp* 2A **32**
Wenvoe. *V Glam* 2C **65**
Weobley. *Here* 3B **40**
Weobley Marsh. *Here* 3B **40**
Wern. *Gwyn* 3A **14**
Wern. *Powy* 1C **59**
(nr. Brecon)
Wern. *Powy* 3D **25**
(nr. Guilsfield)
Wern. *Powy* 3A **24**
(nr. Llangadfon)
Wern. *Powy* 2D **25**
(nr. Llanymynech)
Wernffrwd. *Swan* 3A **56**
Wernyrheolydd. *Mon* 1A **60**
Wervin. *Ches* 3B **10**
West Aberthaw. *V Glam* 3B **64**
West Bank. *Hal* 2C **11**
Westbrook. *Here* 1D **49**
Westbury. *Shrp* 1A **32**
Westbury-on-Severn. *Glos* 1D **61**
Westbury on Trym. *Bris* 2C **67**
West Cross. *Swan* 1B **62**
West Derby. *Mers* 1A **10**
West End. *N Som* 3B **66**
West End. *S Glo* 1D **67**
Westerleigh. *S Glo* 2D **67**
West Felton. *Shrp* 2A **26**
West Harptree. *Bath* 3C **67**
West Hewish. *N Som* 3A **66**
Westhide. *Here* 1C **51**
West Hill. *N Som* 2B **66**
Westhope. *Here* 3B **40**
Westhope. *Shrp* 3B **32**
West Kirby. *Mers* 2D **9**
Westleigh. *G Man* 1D **11**
Westley. *Shrp* 1A **32**
Weston. *Bath* 3D **67**
Weston. *Ches* 2D **19**
Weston. *Hal* 2C **11**
Weston. *Here* 3A **40**
Weston. *Shrp* 2C **33**
(nr. Bridgnorth)
Weston. *Shrp* 1A **40**
(nr. Knighton)
Weston. *Shrp* 2C **27**
(nr. Wem)
Weston Beggard. *Here* 1C **51**
Westoncommon. *Shrp* 2B **26**

Weston-in-Gordano. *N Som* 2B **66**
Weston Lullingfields. *Shrp* 2B **26**
Weston Rhyn. *Shrp* 1D **25**
Weston-super-Mare. *N Som* 3A **66**
Weston under Penyard. *Here* 3D **51**
Westra. *V Glam* 2C **65**
West Town. *Bath* 3C **67**
West Town. *N Som* 3B **66**
West Wick. *N Som* 3A **66**
West Williamston. *Pemb* 2D **53**
Wettenhall. *Ches* 1D **19**
Weythel. *Powy* 3D **39**
Wharton. *Ches* 1D **19**
Wharton. *Here* 3C **41**
Whatmore. *Shrp* 1D **41**
Wheathill. *Shrp* 3D **33**
Wheelock. *Ches* 2D **19**
Wheelock Heath. *Ches* 2D **19**
Whelston. *Flin* 3D **9**
Whiston. *Mers* 1B **10**
Whitbourne. *Here* 3D **41**
Whitby. *Ches* 3A **10**
Whitbyheath. *Ches* 3A **10**
Whitchurch. *Bath* 3D **67**
Whitchurch. *Card* 2C **65**
Whitchurch. *Here* 1C **61**
Whitchurch. *Pemb* 3A **42**
Whitchurch. *Shrp* 3C **19**
Whitcot. *Shrp* 2A **32**
Whitcott Keysett. *Shrp* 3D **31**
Whitebrook. *Mon* 2C **61**
Whitechurch. *Pemb* 2A **44**
Whitecroft. *Glos* 2D **61**
Whitegate. *Ches* 1D **19**
Whitehaven. *Shrp* 2D **25**
White Mill. *Carm* 3D **45**
White Rocks. *Here* 3B **50**
White Stone. *Here* 1C **51**
Whitfield. *S Glo* 3D **61**
Whitford. *Flin* 3C **9**
Whitland. *Carm* 1B **54**
Whitney. *Here* 1D **49**
Whittingslow. *Shrp* 3B **32**
Whittington. *Shrp* 1A **26**
Whitton. *Powy* 2D **39**
Whitton. *Shrp* 1C **41**
Whixall. *Shrp* 1C **27**
Whyle. *Here* 2C **41**
Wibdon. *Glos* 3C **61**
Wick. *S Glo* 2D **67**
Wick. *V Glam* 2A **64**
Wick St Lawrence. *N Som* 3A **66**
Wickwar. *S Glo* 1D **67**
Widnes. *Hal* 2C **11**
Wigmore. *Here* 2B **40**
Wilcott. *Shrp* 3A **26**
Wilderspool. *Warr* 2D **11**
Wilkesley. *Ches* 3D **19**
Willaston. *Ches* 3D **19**
(nr. Crewe)
Willaston. *Ches* 3A **10**
(nr. Neston)
Willersley. *Here* 1A **50**
Willey. *Shrp* 2D **33**
Willington Corner. *Ches* 1C **19**
Willoughbridge. *Staf* 3D **19**
Willsbridge. *S Glo* 2D **67**
Wilmington. *Bath* 3D **67**
Wilson. *Here* 3C **51**
Wincham. *Ches* 3D **11**
Windle Hill. *Ches* 3A **10**
Winford. *N Som* 3C **67**
Winforton. *Here* 1D **49**
Winnal Common. *Here* 2B **50**
Winnington. *Ches* 3D **11**
Winnington. *Staf* 1D **27**

Winscombe. *N Som* 3B **66**
Winsford. *Ches* 1D **19**
Winsh-wen. *Swan* 3B **56**
Winterbourne. *S Glo* 1D **67**
Winterley. *Ches* 2D **19**
Winwick. *Warr* 1D **11**
Wirswall. *Ches* 3C **19**
Wistanstow. *Shrp* 3B **32**
Wistanswick. *Shrp* 2D **27**
Wistaston. *Ches* 2D **19**
Wiston. *Pemb* 1D **53**
Withington. *Here* 1C **51**
Withington. *Shrp* 3C **27**
Withington Marsh. *Here* 1C **51**
Wixhill. *Shrp* 2C **27**
Wolferlow. *Here* 2D **41**
Wolf's Castle. *Pemb* 3C **43**
Wolfsdale. *Pemb* 3C **43**
Wollaston. *Shrp* 3A **26**
Wollerton. *Shrp* 1D **27**
Wolverley. *Shrp* 1B **26**
Wolvesnewton. *Mon* 3B **60**
Womaston. *Powy* 2D **39**
Wood. *Pemb* 3B **42**
Woodbank. *Ches* 3A **10**
Woodchurch. *Mers* 2D **9**
Woodcroft. *Glos* 3C **61**
Woodford. *Glos* 3D **61**
Woodhill. *N Som* 2B **66**
Woodhill. *Shrp* 3D **33**
Woodhouses. *Ches* 3C **11**
Woodlane. *Shrp* 2D **27**
Woods Eaves. *Here* 1D **49**
Woodseaves. *Shrp* 1D **27**
Woodstock Slop. *Pemb* 3D **43**
Woofferton. *Shrp* 2C **41**
Woolaston. *Glos* 3C **61**
Woolhope. *Here* 2D **51**
Woollard. *Bath* 3D **67**
Woolley. *Bath* 3D **67**
Woolstaston. *Shrp* 2B **32**
Woolston. *Shrp* 3B **32**
(nr. Church Stretton)
Woolston. *Shrp* 2A **26**
(nr. Oswestry)
Woolston. *Warr* 1D **11**
Woolton. *Mers* 2B **10**
Woonton. *Here* 3A **40**
(nr. Kington)
Woonton. *Here* 2C **41**
(nr. Leominster)
Woore. *Shrp* 3D **19**
Wootton. *Shrp* 1B **40**
(nr. Ludlow)
Wootton. *Shrp* 2A **26**
(nr. Oswestry)
Worldsend. *Shrp* 2B **32**
Worle. *N Som* 3A **66**
Worleston. *Ches* 2D **19**
Wormbridge. *Here* 2B **50**
Wormelow Tump. *Here* 2B **50**
Wormsley. *Here* 1B **50**
Worsley. *G Man* 1D **11**
Worthen. *Shrp* 1A **32**
Worthenbury. *Wrex* 3B **18**
Wotherton. *Shrp* 1D **31**
Wraxall. *N Som* 2B **66**
Wrecsam. *Wrex* 2A **18**
Wrenbury. *Ches* 3C **19**
Wrentnall. *Shrp* 1B **32**
Wrexham. *Wrex* 2A **18**
Wrexham Industrial Estate.
Wrex 3A **18**
Wrickton. *Shrp* 3D **33**
Wrinehill. *Staf* 3D **19**
Wrington. *N Som* 3B **66**
Wrockwardine. *Telf* 3D **27**

Wroxeter. *Shrp* 1C **33**
Wybunbury. *Ches* 3D **19**
Wyesham. *Mon* 1C **61**
Wyke. *Shrp* 1D **33**
Wyke, The. *Shrp* 1D **33**
Wykey. *Shrp* 2A **26**
Wyndham. *B'end* 3A **58**
Wyson. *Here* 2C **41**

Y

Yanley. *N Som* 3C **67**
Yardro. *Powy* 3D **39**
Yarkhill. *Here* 1D **51**
Yarpole. *Here* 2B **40**
Yarsop. *Here* 1B **50**
Yate. *S Glo* 1D **67**
Yatton. *Here* 2B **40**
(nr. Leominster)
Yatton. *Here* 2D **51**
(nr. Ross-on-Wye)
Yatton. *N Som* 3B **66**
Yazor. *Here* 1B **50**
Y Bala. *Gwyn* 1A **24**
Y Bont-Faen. *V Glam* 2A **64**
Y Dref. *Gwyn* 1D **21**
Y Drenewydd. *Powy* 2C **31**
Yearsett. *Here* 3D **41**
Yeaton. *Shrp* 3B **26**
Yerbeston. *Pemb* 2D **53**
Y Felinheli. *Gwyn* 1A **14**
Y Fenni. *Mon* 1A **60**
Y Ferwig. *Cdgn* 1A **44**
Y Fflint. *Flin* 3D **9**
Y Ffor. *Gwyn* 1C **21**
Y Gelli Gandryll. *Powy* 1D **49**
Ynysboeth. *Rhon* 3B **58**
Ynysddu. *Cphy* 3C **59**
Ynysforgan. *Swan* 3B **56**
Ynyshir. *Rhon* 3B **58**
Ynyslas. *Cdgn* 2B **28**
Ynysmaerdy. *Neat* 3C **57**
Ynysmeudwy. *Neat* 2C **57**
Ynystawe. *Swan* 2B **56**
Ynyswen. *Powy* 1D **57**
Ynys-wen. *Rhon* 3A **58**
Ynys y Barri. *V Glam* 3C **65**
Ynysybwl. *Rhon* 3B **58**
Ynysy]maerdy. *Rhon* 1B **64**
Yockleton. *Shrp* 3B **26**
Yorkley. *Glos* 2D **61**
Yorton. *Shrp* 2C **27**
Yorton Heath. *Shrp* 2C **27**
Yr Hob. *Flin* 2A **18**
Y Rhws. *V Glam* 3B **64**
Yr Wyddgrug. *Flin* 1D **17**
Ysbyty Cynfyn. *Cdgn* 1C **37**
Ysbyty Ifan. *Cnwy* 3D **15**
Ysbyty Ystwyth. *Cdgn* 1C **37**
Ysceifiog. *Flin* 3C **9**
Yspitty. *Carm* 3A **56**
Ystalyfera. *Neat* 2C **57**
Ystrad. *Rhon* 3A **58**
Ystrad Aeron. *Cdgn* 3A **36**
Ystradfellte. *Powy* 1A **58**
Ystradffin. *Carm* 1C **47**
Ystradgynlais. *Powy* 1C **57**
Ystradmeurig. *Cdgn* 2C **37**
Ystrad Mynach. *Cphy* 3C **59**
Ystradowen. *Neat* 1C **57**
Ystradowen. *V Glam* 2B **64**
Ystumtuen. *Cdgn* 1C **37**
Y Trallwng. *Powy* 1C **31**
Y Waun. *Wrex* 1D **25**

CITY & TOWN CENTRE PLANS (Cynlluniau Canol Dinasoedd a Threfi)

Reference to Town Plans

MOTORWAY	M4	BUS STATION	
MOTORWAY UNDER CONSTRUCTION		CAR PARK (Selection of)	P
MOTORWAY JUNCTIONS WITH NUMBERS	4 5	CHURCH	†
Unlimited Interchange 4		CITY WALL	
Limited Interchange 5		FERRY (Vehicular)	
PRIMARY ROUTE	A55	(Foot only)	
PRIMARY ROUTE JUNCTION WITH NUMBER	15	GOLF COURSE	
DUAL CARRIAGEWAYS		HELIPORT	
CLASS A ROAD	A48	HOSPITAL	H
CLASS B ROAD	B4246	INFORMATION CENTRE	i
MAJOR ROADS UNDER CONSTRUCTION		LIGHTHOUSE	
MAJOR ROADS PROPOSED		MARKET	
MINOR ROADS		NATIONAL TRUST PROPERTY (Open)	NT
RESTRICTED ACCESS		(Restricted opening)	NT
PEDESTRIANIZED ROAD & MAIN FOOTWAY		(National Trust of Scotland)	NTS NTS
ONE WAY STREETS		PARK & RIDE	P+
TOLL	TOLL	PLACE OF INTEREST	
RAILWAY AND B.R. STATION		POLICE STATION	▲
UNDERGROUND / METRO & D.L.R. STATION	DLR	POST OFFICE	★
LEVEL CROSSING AND TUNNEL		SHOPPING AREA (Main street and precinct)	
TRAM STOP AND ONE WAY TRAM STOP		SHOPMOBILITY	
BUILT-UP AREA		TOILET	▼
ABBEY, CATHEDRAL, PRIORY ETC.	†	VIEWPOINT	

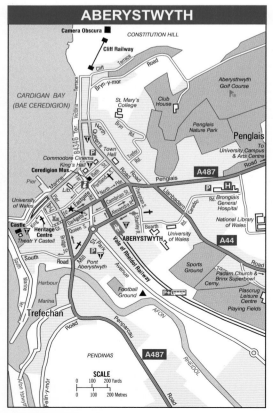

ABERYSTWYTH

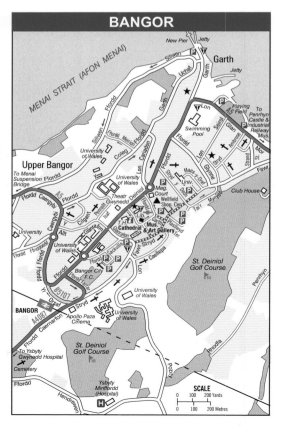

BANGOR

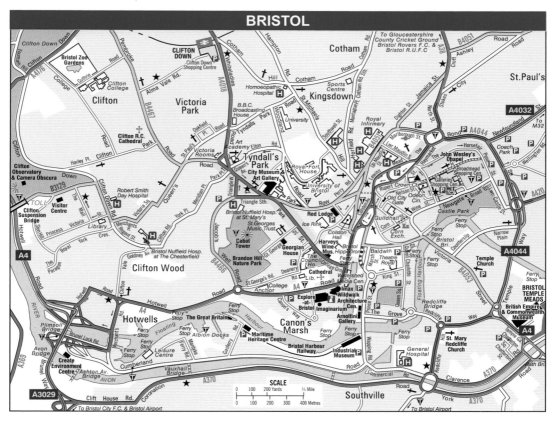

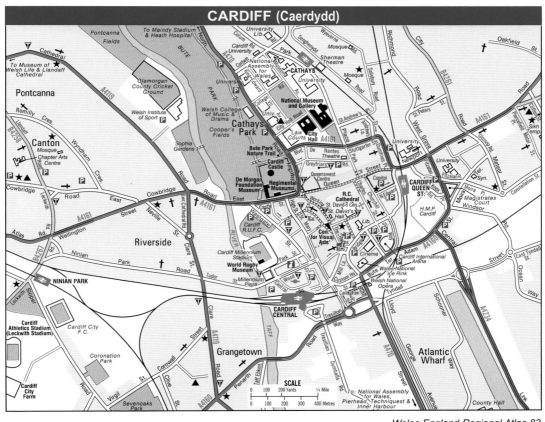

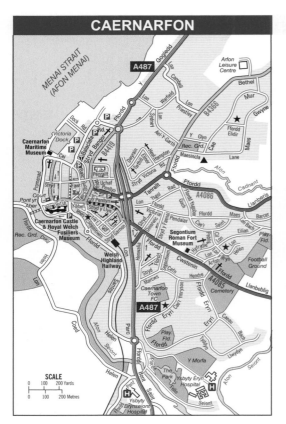

CAERNARFON

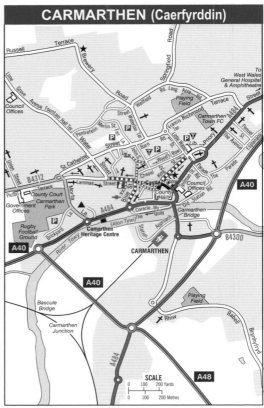

CARMARTHEN (Caerfyrddin)

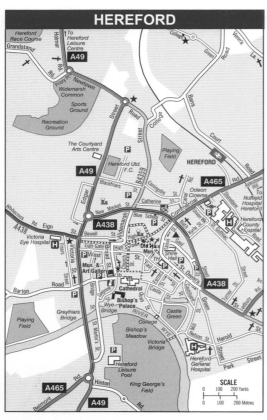

HEREFORD

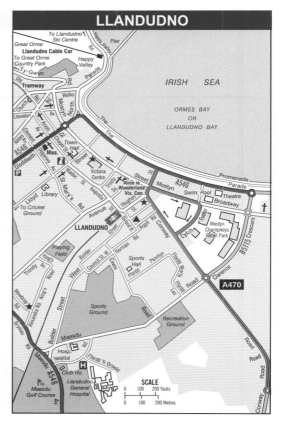

LLANDUDNO

LIVERPOOL

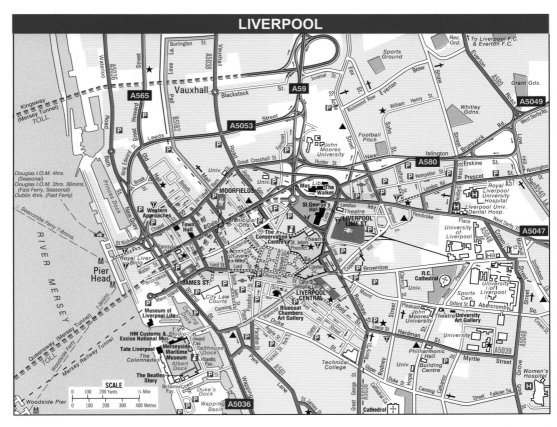

LLANELLI

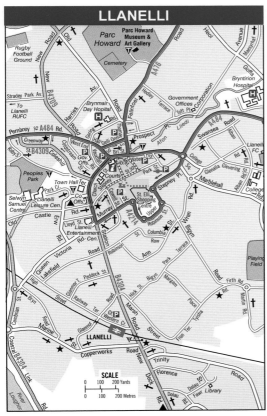

MERTHYR TYDFIL (Merthyr Tudful)

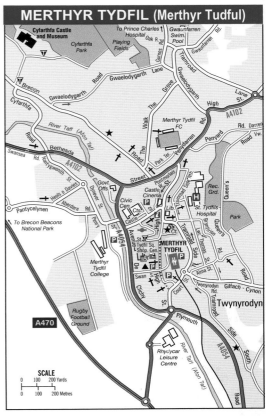

NEWPORT (Casnewydd)

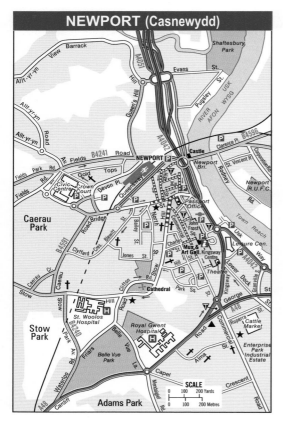

SHREWSBURY

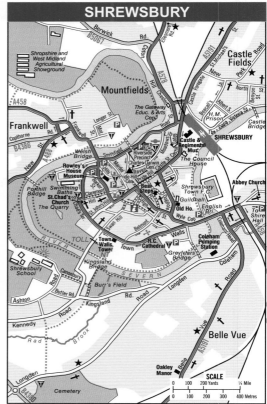

SWANSEA (Abertawe)

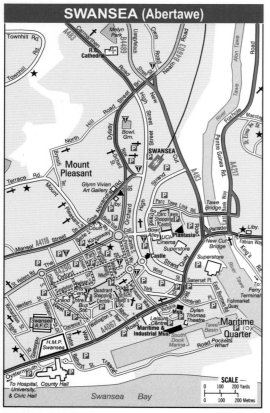

WREXHAM (Wrecsam)

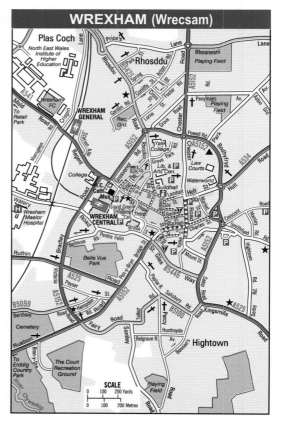

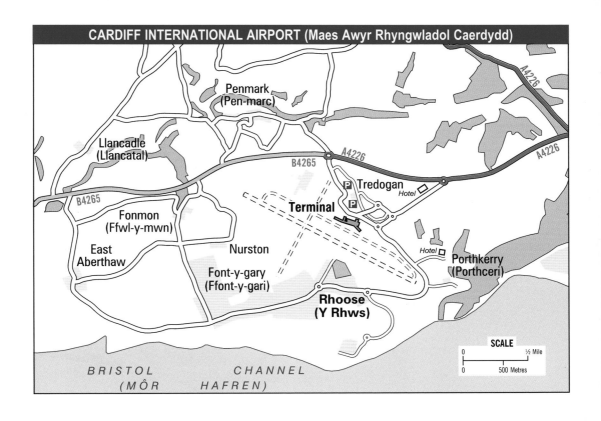

CARDIFF INTERNATIONAL AIRPORT (Maes Awyr Rhyngwladol Caerdydd)

Penmark
(Pen-marc)

Llancadle
(Llancatal)

A4226

B4265

A4226

A4226

B4265

Tredogan
P
Hotel

Terminal
P

Fonmon
(Ffwl-y-mwn)

East
Aberthaw

Nurston

Hotel
Porthkerry
(Porthceri)

Font-y-gary
(Ffont-y-gari)

Rhoose
(Y Rhws)

SCALE
0 ½ Mile
0 500 Metres

BRISTOL   CHANNEL
(MÔR   HAFREN)

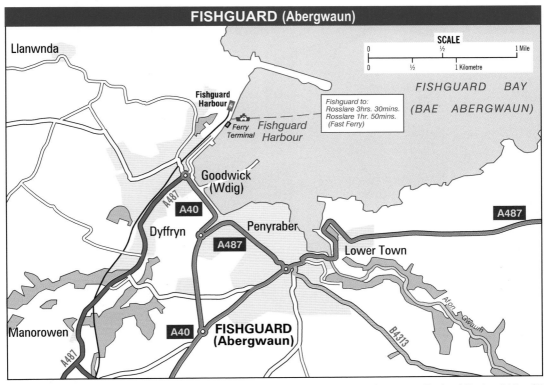

FISHGUARD (Abergwaun)

Llanwnda

SCALE
0 ½ 1 Mile
0 ½ 1 Kilometre

FISHGUARD   BAY
(BAE   ABERGWAUN)

Fishguard
Harbour

Ferry
Terminal

*Fishguard
Harbour*

Fishguard to:
Rosslare 3hrs. 30mins.
Rosslare 1hr. 50mins.
(Fast Ferry)

Goodwick
(Wdig)

A487

A40

Dyffryn

Penyraber

A487

A487

A487

Lower Town

Manorowen

A40

**FISHGUARD
(Abergwaun)**

B4313

Afon Gwauti

A487

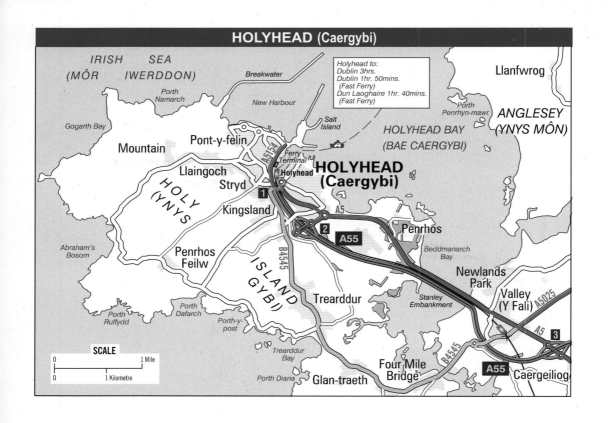

HOLYHEAD (Caergybi)

IRISH SEA
(MÔR IWERDDON)

Breakwater

New Harbour

Holyhead to:
Dublin 3hrs.
Dublin 1hr. 50mins.
(Fast Ferry)
Dun Laoghaire 1hr. 40mins.
(Fast Ferry)

Llanfwrog

Porth
Namarch

Porth
Penrhyn-mawr

Salt
Island

ANGLESEY
(YNYS MÔN)

Gogarth Bay

HOLYHEAD BAY
(BAE CAERGYBI)

Mountain

Pont-y-felin

Ferry
Terminal

Holyhead

**HOLYHEAD
(Caergybi)**

Llaingoch

Stryd

HOLY
(YNYS

Kingsland

A5

Penrhos

A55

Beddmanrach
Bay

Abraham's
Bosom

Penrhos
Feilw

ISLAND
GYBI)

Newlands
Park

Valley
(Y Fali)

A5025

Trearddur

Stanley
Embankment

A5

Porth
Ruffydd

Porth
Dafarch

Porth-y-
post

Trearddur
Bay

Four Mile
Bridge

Caergeiliog

A55

SCALE

0 ————— 1 Mile

0 ————— 1 Kilometre

Porth Diana

Glan-traeth

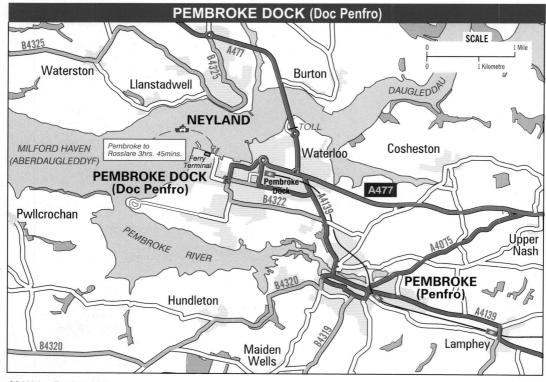

PEMBROKE DOCK (Doc Penfro)

B4325

Waterston

Llanstadwell

A477

B4325

Burton

DAUGLEDDAU

SCALE

0 ————— 1 Mile

0 ————— 1 Kilometre

MILFORD HAVEN
(ABERDAUGLEDDYF)

NEYLAND

TOLL

Pembroke to
Rosslare 3hrs. 45mins.

Ferry
Terminal

Waterloo

Cosheston

**PEMBROKE DOCK
(Doc Penfro)**

Pembroke
Dock

A477

B4322

A4139

Pwllcrochan

PEMBROKE
RIVER

B4320

Upper
Nash

A4075

Hundleton

B4320

B4319

Maiden
Wells

**PEMBROKE
(Penfró)**

Lamphey

A4139